THE
BUCK
PROPS
HERE!

*For Alana who introduced me to rugby,
and Gareth for giving me an opportunity*

THE BUCK PROPS HERE!

ANTHONY BUCHANAN

WITH GERAINT THOMAS

First impression: 2021

© Copyright Anthony Buchanan,
Geraint Thomas and Y Lolfa Cyf., 2021

The publishers wish to acknowledge the support of
the Books Council of Wales

Cover image © Andrew Richards
Cover design: Sion Ilar

ISBN: 978 1 912631 34 6

Published and printed in Wales
on paper from well-maintained forests by
Y Lolfa Cyf., Talybont, Ceredigion SY24 5HE
website www.ylolfa.com
e-mail ylolfa@ylolfa.com
tel 01970 832 304
fax 832 782

Contents

Foreword
Gareth Jenkins

WHEN ALAN LEWIS took over as coach of Llanelli RFC in 1982 – we were both young players who had suffered career-ending injuries – he asked me to join him to oversee the forwards. We quickly realised that we had to recruit a new group of players – our current side had been there when I had played for Llanelli and were getting too long in the tooth. It was a case of going out and looking for new players, with a particular emphasis on second rows and props.

One prospect who caught my eye was this young player from Ystradgynlais – he's running all around the field, he's a big-set boy, he's a ball handler who enjoys the open spaces, he's very aggressive in his ball carrying, but he's playing Number 8. His name was Anthony Buchanan. He impressed me, he had potential, but he would have to go into the front row.

We had a chat with Anthony and said we were prepared to give him a chance at prop – if he committed to this opportunity over the next few months, by playing that position with his club, we would then give him a game with Llanelli. We kept in touch and he put everything into it. Going from a goalkeeper, where he started off his sporting career, to a prop isn't the easiest transition in the world, but he committed himself fully to it.

His big chance came in a derby game against Swansea, down at St Helen's, when we picked him on the loose-head.

He didn't see much of the game, or the ball, as his head was stuck in the pitch for most of it – he was playing against a big promising prop, Gareth John, who had international potential. He had an outing but he really dug in and ended up impressing all of us with his strength of character, tenacity and his stubbornness not to be beaten.

We included him in our squad for the rest of the season. That's where his journey with the Scarlets started. It reflects the way Welsh rugby was back in the day; before the regions and professionalism it offered an opportunity for anybody. It's very different now, it's very categorised; if you're not identified by the time you are 17 or 18, the likelihood is that you are not going to progress.

While we were looking at Anthony there was another young prop, from Pembrokeshire, who was making waves at the time, by the name of Brian Williams. I went down to watch him play for Narberth. One thing was obvious, he had an engine and a half. There was no doubt that he would make an impact on the game but, for a prop, he was very slight. I was looking to build a forward pack which could hold its own against any team in Wales in the front row, so we ignored Brian and went for Anthony. It turned out to be the correct decision because Anthony developed into being a very, very good prop who ended up playing at the Rugby World Cup.

Brian didn't turn out too badly either, but he was a typical Neath player – they designed their teams around aggression and physicality. I was looking to create a good platform in the scrums and lineouts, to play free-flowing rugby. My vision of a pack was very different from Ron Waldron's. He was looking for a very aggressive, marauding bunch of players who intimidated the opposition into submission.

Alongside Anthony we recruited a Wales Youth cap from New Dock Stars called Laurance Delaney; Phil May and Alun Davies, who were two young players coming out of Llanelli

Grammar School, and we had been told about a big, big lump of a young man from Porthcawl, called Russell Cornelius. We had the cornerstone of a pack that would serve the club so well for the next ten years.

Without a doubt, it was a huge learning curve for Anthony but he had tenacity and ambition. He was the type of boy who would never give up, in rugby or in life. He was a very determined and focused individual. He was prepared to learn, and he did learn. Within 18 months the whole group of front five players which we had recruited were all shaping up into a useful unit. Within two years it was obvious that Anthony was going to have international recognition; there was no doubt in my mind.

He had learnt the hard lessons, he had done his apprenticeship and had started to establish himself as a very mobile and scrummaging prop.

When international recognition came it was more than deserved. He never let Wales down, and to have played in the inaugural World Cup and reached third place was fantastic for his career. The only disappointment for Anthony is that he never had the chance to play for Wales in the National Stadium, because he deserved that.

He should have had more caps in my opinion, but there were far fewer international games when he played and there was this huge competition for places. Back in the day you didn't have four regions, there were 16 first-class teams and there were good props throughout Welsh rugby. If you had a good game on the Saturday, you could be an international the week after! It was as precarious as that. When Anthony was playing there must have been half a dozen props who were all being selected depending on the emotion of the selectors and the coaches. There were a lot of boys who had around ten caps each. Today it's very much the case that if you break through to the international side you establish yourself and get 30 or 40 caps. Not many front row players would have reached that number previously, apart from Graham Price who was a world-class player.

*

Anthony had a tremendous career with Llanelli, playing well over 200 games, and when the time came I knew I had to handle his retirement from the game carefully. It's about creating an environment of respect, and when these boys were coming to the end of their careers it was important that they were prepared properly for it and that they understood the reasoning behind it. Those conversations were very important. When players retire from the game, having put as much into it as these boys had, their consideration has to be taken into account. It's a two-way street.

Anthony was still a good prop, but Ricky Evans emerged and became an international player very quickly. It was difficult for Anthony but he did understand and was prepared to accept that Ricky became a priority selection.

*

When Alan Lewis called it a day – we were amateurs remember, and he felt the pressure and responsibility of the role, combined with his teaching career, was too much and so he resigned – I became coach of the club, as opposed to assistant coach.

One of the first steps I took was to create a team management group, because one of the pressures Alan had experienced, every Monday night, was having to go in front of the main club committee of 11 and have a discussion around the team selection and the issues which went with it – half his coaching time was taken up with committee meetings.

I set up the matchday committee, with two representatives of the main committee who could report back instead of my having to spend the whole evening in the committee room. I also created the role of match secretary to take responsibility for travel arrangements, to deal with phone calls around selection and pass on details to the players. It became a very important role within the organisation. It was a significant step forward back in those days, and was needed because the game was evolving pretty quickly. The first guy appointed was Alan James. He had been a great player for the club – I had played alongside him – and he had the qualities for a very difficult role. He did a fantastic job – everyone respected Alan and I remember Anthony telling me on several occasions how he admired Alan for the way he managed things and behaved, how he maintained discipline.

When, after three years, Alan felt the time had to come to step down – it was a time-consuming role – it coincided with Anthony retiring as a player, and I suggested that it was a role which would fit him if he considered taking it on. He gave it some consideration and then accepted – it was the beginning of the team manager role which he fulfilled for 15 years.

Anthony was always a balanced boy, he had common sense, he was a player who understood how players thought and behaved, he had lived the life of a player and understood a player's mentality.

I ended up having a long coaching career because of the people around me and my own view of rugby and commitment to the game. Anthony became a significant colleague of mine. My relationship with Anthony is probably the longest I've enjoyed in my life, and it's built upon respect, regard and admiration for the type of man he is and what he's achieved.

It was important that we saw things the same way, that he managed the environment the way we wanted it to be, and Anthony was very much on the same wavelength as myself all the way through the journey. There's no doubt at all about that. You need to make sure that the team manager becomes the go-to person who you are comfortable with – I had enough on my plate doing all the other bits and pieces.

Anthony did say that if there was going to be a problem then he would need me to come into it. I agreed, but did say that I didn't want to be pestered either! As it turned out, on the odd occasion that required further intervention – it wasn't very often – he used to call me and say, 'We need to get the bogeyman out.'

The number of occasions I had to be brought in was very rare, which is a testimony to Anthony's abilities as he developed into his team manager role.

When I left to coach Wales, and Phil Davies came in to replace me, I felt I was leaving a safe pair of hands in Anthony. However, for whatever reason, Anthony decided to step down and return to Ystradgynlais, and it's no coincidence in my book that a lot of things started to unravel and we lost all our games in Europe the following season.

When I was sacked by Wales – it was humiliating and very poorly dealt with but these things happen and you have to deal with them and get on with your life – I took a couple of months out before being invited back to the club. I had no appetite to go back to coaching; I had done 25 years, and I wanted something else in my journey. I suggested Nigel Davies be considered and he was and was appointed.

I then spoke to Huw Evans and the committee about creating a sustainable development model – if the Scarlets were going to have a future, we had to have the ability to develop on a year-to-year basis young talent coming through to the region. The committee agreed and tasked me with making that happen – this was 15 years ago.

I knew exactly what was needed, and so the first person I turned to was Anthony.

We had just become a region and needed to regionalise the Scarlets. We had to shape and drive the region's rugby philosophy. This was something I took upon myself to accomplish, and my lieutenant was Anthony. I spoke to him and he still had the appetite, and ambition, and was more than happy to come back.

At the time the Premiership clubs were receiving a fortune from the WRU – something in the region of £150,000 per club – but there was no relationship between young player development and the clubs. I wanted to model Llanelli differently. This meant that if we had good youngsters, I wanted them to play senior rugby at 17, 18 and 19 years old on a Saturday. I wanted them to feel uncomfortable in order to keep their development going. Anthony shared my philosophy and took it upon himself to develop Llanelli RFC into a feeder club for the Scarlets.

It worked and Anthony, to be fair to him, drove it through the time and commitment he put into it. He made the model work and the Scarlets are completely indebted to him for the work he put in to developing a model for the academies coming through into the Premiership. He set the standards, 15 years ago, of how the Premiership could become the pathway for young players coming through to international level.

*

Time goes on and people have become confused over the regional philosophy. It was rolled out by David Moffett and within months he had walked away from it. People made up the regional philosophy to suit their own region – they all behaved differently and had different ways of thinking about it. It started off being governed by the WRU, but then it stepped back, and left the regions to behave as they felt they needed to. We took the view of regionalising the Scarlets in a different way to the other regions – whether that was a mistake or not I do not know. They should have started off centrally by laying down how the regions should work within their regional boundaries; it would have prevented a lot of problems rather than creating them.

Anthony modelled Llanelli in a manner I believe Welsh rugby should have modelled the Premiership, but it never happened.

Anthony then approached me and said he was going to try something different, and a lot of people had approached him to try and get him on to the WRU board. He believed that the Premiership should have a better relationship with the regions. It was a great move for Anthony because he had done everything else. It was his chance to have his moment in the sun, and what a great job he made of it.

*

And so to our latest challenge. The WRU made an awful decision a few years ago and devalued the Premiership as the head of the community game in Wales. The Premiership, across the 12 big clubs in Welsh rugby historically, cannot disappear from the game. It cannot disappear from the fabric of Welsh rugby, but the then WRU CEO Martin Phillips, and board member Gareth Davies, made the disastrous decision which denigrated the great clubs of Wales into community rugby clubs, which they never should have been. The Premiership should always be linked to the regions. There has to be a place where young players can play a high standard of competitive rugby.

If Llanelli ever became a community club it wouldn't be sustainable. When we became Llanelli Scarlets the facility of Stradey Park was sold into a partnership with Carmarthenshire County Council, and the multimillion pound asset went into building the new stadium, Parc y Scarlets. It's an international stadium, but it's there because our asset of over 150 years was sold to build it.

Llanelli's relationship with the Scarlets currently allows us to play on Parc y Scarlets – it's a joint ground. The problem we face is we haven't got a lot of opportunity to generate an income and we are very dependant on the WRU. The new payment structure, after they devalued us down to the community game, means we only get £50,000 a year – you cannot run a club like Llanelli on that.

There are major political issues going on and Anthony has taken it upon himself to involve people like myself, Rupert Moon and a few others to try and ensure the name of Llanelli Rugby Football Club, and the history it carries, remains a part of the Scarlets and their future. I have no doubt that Anthony will rise to the challenge once more.

Gareth Jenkins
Llanelli, Scarlets and Wales

CHAPTER 1

Football Crazy

I DOUBT THAT there are many international rugby players around who received the 'dap' – an instrument of punishment made from the sole of a gym shoe – across the backside for refusing to play the game in school. I did on a number of occasions.

Growing up in Cwmtwrch, at the top end of the upper Swansea Valley, my first and last love was football. It was a passion passed down from my father and grandfather who were born and bred a goal kick or so away from White Hart Lane, the home of Tottenham Hotspur, and nothing could change that. Rugby was not even on the horizon for discussion when I was a boy, as far as my family were concerned.

Our PE teacher at Maesydderwen School was Gareth Thomas, affectionately known as Snowy. A former outside-half for the All Whites, he tried his best to get me to play rugby but I did not have any interest in the game whatsoever. On one occasion he found a group of boys playing football on the school fields and immediately confiscated the ball. And that was the last anyone ever saw of it!

Maesydderwen had a fine reputation and produced quite a few schoolboy internationals. I suppose Snowy must have seen something in me. On several occasions he would single me out. 'Where's your kit, boy?' he would holler with disdain. My reply, which was always, 'I've left it at home, Sir,' would elicit the inevitable tap on the backside with the dreaded dap.

I stuck to my guns as schoolboy rugby was played on a Saturday morning, which clashed with my junior football, so there was never any chance of my picking up rugby in school – I didn't even watch Wales play on the television back then. I was 22 years old before I played my first game of rugby.

Such was my love of football that it also scuppered my involvement in the family business. My grandmother on my mother's side had a butcher's shop in Lower Cwmtwrch, and the family wanted me to take over the business one day. So, when I turned 15, I was offered an apprenticeship. But, to the immense disappointment of my family, I turned it down because it meant working Saturday mornings, and I was not going to give up my football.

*

My grandfather, Joseph Buchanan, was from Burnt Oak, a suburb in the Edgware district of London. He was a piano maker and worked for one of the top firms in the country – you could say my grandfather was a piano maker and I ended up, as a prop forward, being a piano shifter!

He was a massive Spurs fan and used to sit near the manager, Bill Nicholson, at home games, after being given an honorary seat for life at White Hart Lane due to his support for the club – he was on the committee of the supporters' club.

That love of Spurs was passed down to my father, Jack Buchanan, although he later switched allegiance to the Swans and became a vice president of the supporters' club. He used to take my brother and me, as kids, down to the Vetch Field to watch home games.

My grandmother, Flo, used to work at Lord's Cricket Ground, so my summer holidays were spent watching the game at the home of cricket and helping her collect the members' cushions from the old wooden seats after the close of play.

Although I enjoyed watching the game, I never took to playing cricket for whatever reason.

When he was 19 or 20 my father left London behind for a job with Smiths Industries in Ystradgynlais. The factory made clocks, and so was known to everyone locally as the Tick Tock. He started off as a toolmaker and ended up as a production manager.

There were around 2,000 people working there at the time and it even had its own sports teams and social club. As you can imagine, there were plenty of relationships formed amongst the employees and my parents were no exception, as my father first met my mother, Margaret Williams, when she worked there on the assembly line.

They married on 7 June 1948 which was Derby day. One of the horses running was called My Love, and it won and made quite a sum of money for my uncles at the wedding who had placed a bet. I was born in Neath General Hospital on 30 June 1955, the youngest child, with Robert being the eldest and my sister Beverley the middle child.

*

As children interested in football and growing up in the area, we were extremely fortunate that Albert Turner dedicated himself to running Cwmphil Rovers, the junior section of Cwm Wanderers in Lower Cwmtwrch. Cwm Wanderers were phenomenally successful in the Neath & District League and further afield in west Wales.

We would meet outside his house on Saturday mornings and go off and play the various towns and villages across the area and, although it was a competitive circuit, we were quite successful as a team and produced some great players.

I was not the only future rugby international to play in the soccer team, as the likes of Alun Donovan (Cardiff and Wales) and Kevin Hopkins (Swansea and Wales) also played for Cwm, and Huw Richards (Neath and Wales) also played football for the opposition.

My chosen position was between the posts. I was just drawn to playing goalkeeper. It was not a case of the hopeless kid being told to go in goal, I chose to play there. Most kids have their heroes and mine was a player called Gerwyn Howells who played in goal for Cwm Wanderers. He was nicknamed Tarzan; he didn't have a chimp as a friend but he had long hair and a good physique.

I would play for Cwmphil Rovers in the morning and go and watch my childhood heroes, Cwm Wanderers, in the Neath & District League in the afternoon. My aim back then was to get into the first team.

*

We used to play in the Norwich City colours, socks, shorts, and shirts, as Albert was originally from Norwich and he had contacts there. Scouts used to come down to watch us play and there was an opportunity for us to improve ourselves. A local boy, Doug Evans, went on to play for Norwich and another, Peter Jones, went up there for trials. My brother was also an exceptional football player and attracted some interest from Leeds United at one stage.

Seeing my peers progress only served to fuel my ambition of doing well in the game.

I must have showed promise at a young age because, when I was 16 years old, I was selected for a trial with Swansea down at the Vetch Field. Unfortunately, it was not quite the stuff of dreams as I let five goals in – I blamed my brother as he kept talking to me from behind the goal. But it did not put me off and I was still determined to play at a higher level.

*

As much as I was crazy about football at this time, horses were my first love. It probably came from the farming family background on my mother's side. As a kid I used to look after horses for others at a nearby stables, until I managed to get my own when I turned 20. He was a Welsh cob who I called Chief – it had nothing to do with the Pontypridd Number 8 Dale McIntosh!

Each morning I used to go to the stables to feed and muck-out, run to school, sometimes late, resulting in a telling-off; then, as soon as the bell rang for home time, I would be straight back to the stables. I even smelled like a horse – my mother used to go absolutely nuts with me.

Tragically, all that changed one fateful day which I will never forget. I used to go out with the Banwen Hunt but, on one particular occasion, I couldn't go out as Chief threw a shoe. The blacksmith came and shod him, so I thought I would exercise him before going to play football.

When I returned I led him to the stable and took his saddle off and felt – as I remember to this day – something was not quite right. I could feel him shaking, and as I turned he started collapsing. Now I was on my own and he was over 16 hands tall but I managed to get him back up and I held him. There was no one else around and I could feel him going away from me as I tired – I knew that if I let him go to the floor he would be gone. In the end I had to let go and run for help, but by the time it arrived he had died – I was heartbroken.

It was more than likely a twisted gut or something, but what amazed me was the vet sent me a bill for £10 just for telling me my horse was dead.

I just could not face being around horses for a long time after that. Talking to different people since, it's strange how common such a thing is. I met up with Doddie Weir years later at a World Rugby event and we sat down at a table with our wives and spoke about different things before realising that we both had a love of horses. He told me that he was similar inasmuch as it was also a turn of fate that brought him into rugby.

In my case it was losing my horse – it turned me off horses straight away, it finished me. In all likelihood, if I hadn't lost Chief in that way, I would be in some stables mucking out right now instead of writing this book, as I would never have had time for rugby.

*

Our home pitch was fairly unique, as it had a massive slope that looked like something out of the Gren calendars which are famous for their cartoon illustrations. It ran from touchline to touchline, so one goalpost was six foot six and the other was seven foot six! One thing that I had to my advantage was that I only lived 50 yards down the road, so I could practice on it a lot and understood the slope better than most. I knew exactly how the field would play when I kicked or threw the ball out. When sides used to visit, they would be very disadvantaged.

*

There was a tremendous amount of respect for the committeemen who ran the club back then. They were admired, in their blazers and tie, for being the mainstay of the club. They were held in high regard and when they told you, 'this is how it is', then that was how it was. These were Neil Morgan, Lew Rees, Sammy Moses and chairman Adrian Jones. It was the same at Ystradgynlais Rugby Football Club where you had the three Glyns – Glyn Davies, Glyn Rees and Glyn Edwards – running the show.

I obviously did not know it at the time but this would help me later in life, after I hung up my boots and got involved with the administrative side of rugby.

*

I graduated to Cwm Wanders in my late teens and started off in the second team before breaking into the firsts after a couple of seasons – it was THE moment as I replaced my childhood hero, Tarzan! He was a highly respected goalkeeper and I certainly had to wait for my chance but now it was my time – I had achieved my ambition of playing for Cwm.

I firmly believe that everyone should have an ambition to play at the highest level if they can. And, once they are there, to aim for the next. That trait has stood me in good stead over the years. I have never rested on my laurels and have always wanted to play at the next level up. My philosophy was, 'Get into the team and then have the ambition to play at a higher level.' (After playing for Wales, I wanted to play for the Lions. At the time it was marginal whether I was good enough or not for the 1989 tour to Australia, but it was not to be.)

I did not have to wait long for my chance to step up as I was asked to play for Ystradgynlais AFC in the Welsh League. Unfortunately, that didn't go as well as I would have liked as I let 21 goals in in two games! One was against a Cardiff City side in the Brains Cup, which we lost 11–0, but they had around five first-team players. Then we went up to Spencer's Steelworks in Newport and got thumped 10–0. I still have a newspaper cutting with the headline 'Tough on Goalkeeper'. None of the goals were my fault if I am honest, and I pointed out to anyone who would listen that there were ten players in front of me before the ball got to me!

Looking back, that gave me a valuable experience of facing a setback in my career and having the determination to learn from it and bounce back.

*

I returned to play for Cwm but refused to drop my head and knuckled down to developing as a player. I must have done well as I was later spotted by some scouts and invited to go down the valley and play for Clydach United, who were a more established Premiership Welsh League side.

As it turned out, I only spent two or three months with Clydach as life had other plans for me. I quit the club and football altogether to try my hand at rugby.

The Clydach United manager at that time, a former Welsh amateur international called Wayne Williams, said he was gutted when I decided to leave because I had more ability than I realised as a goalkeeper and he felt I could have gone further.

I wouldn't say that it was a dream of mine to play football for Wales as a kid, but if you played at a professional level it was a possibility, and I was creeping towards it – with a bit of luck I may have made it but I felt that if I couldn't see it happening for me when I was 22, then it was probably never going to happen for me. I also could not get to grips with all the travelling. There was a lot of travelling involved in the Welsh League – you had to leave really early in the morning for the long trips up north to places like Caersws and Bangor.

But, while the travelling was an issue, the real reason that I decided to turn my back on football and play rugby was love. I had met the girl I would later marry, Alana Edwards, and I wanted to spend more time with her.

Alana Edwards worked behind the bar at Ystradgynlais Rugby Club. She was working her way through teacher training at university in Cardiff – and I still remember the first time I saw her. Do not ask me how, but Alana also felt something for me, and the rugby club soon became the centre of my social life. In fact, it was the social hub of the whole town and surrounds (including Cwmtwrch) back then, and the place to be – the local football clubs did not have their own clubhouses and operated out of pubs. It used to be ram-packed on a Friday, Saturday and Sunday night. If you were not there by 7 o'clock you would not get a seat. If I was away playing football, I used to run home, get changed and run to the club to meet her. They would keep a seat for me, otherwise I would not get in.

I really enjoyed the social side of the club and, as I began spending more time there, I started getting friendly with the rugby boys and Alana's brother, Kevin, who I soon learnt was the tight-head prop and captain of the club. After a few dates I started to realise that her whole family – including parents Euros and Harriet – were life members and absolutely committed to the rugby club.

There was a downside. While I was enjoying myself as a soccer player, I regarded myself as someone who was on the fringe of things, an outsider looking in. It was then that I came to a momentous decision. Casting aside my previously held preconceptions about rugby, I decided to give it a go.

When I went home and told my family that I was going to play rugby I was greeted with shock – everyone, including those at Cwm Wanderers, did a John McEnroe and said, 'You cannot be serious.'

But I stuck to my guns and said, 'I'm going to give it a go.'

*

When you decide to shift your sport like that, you realise that you have to start again from the bottom, and that was fine with me. At Ystradgynlais, that meant the seconds.

I discovered in my first season, 1977/78, that the team was made up of older guys winding down their careers – half of them would have a few before the game, you would go down in the scrum and smell the beer – and the youngsters coming up. I had several lessons from the old heads playing for the seconds – they tried to drag me into every ruck or maul.

When I turned up for my first-ever training session, they asked me what position I played – I did not tell them that I had never played the game before – and I so I said fullback. I was quite fast and could kick a ball after being a goalkeeper.

24

No questions were asked, and I was selected there for the following Saturday. It did not go well. I had not read the game particularly well and was caught out of position on a number of occasions and we got hammered. After the game they said, 'You're not going to be a fullback, you will have to go in the forwards.'

I did not argue and lined up as Number 8 in the next game – I was quite tall at six foot one and looked down on most of the team.

The thing I remember most from my first game at Number 8 is that my ears were burning so much from packing down in the scrum. The following game I tried wearing a scrum cap, but someone caught hold of it and gave me a couple of belts. I soon learned to tape my ears up. I wore a two-inch sticky tape band with one-inch black electrician tape on top for the rest of my career, and always had sticky hair after games.

*

All in all, I took to rugby quite well – I grasped what I had to do and grasped it quickly. One thing I had going for me was, as a goalkeeper, I was already able to catch a ball. That gave me a big advantage when it came to my handling skills – although some people may dispute that!

I was also used to playing football with my head up, as they say, and that gave me the ability to read a game. My time in football may not have prepared me physically, but mentally I was able to look up and see where everyone was and know where to go.

It was mentioned when I started playing for Llanelli that I played the game a lot differently to the other forwards at the time. I played a lot looser game because I could see that there was no point in piling into a ruck when the ball would soon be going the other way. I suppose you would call me today a 'modern' prop. My game was based around catching, running, passing, tackling and being in the game – looking at the game, reading the game and seeing it in front of you. I used to be amazed by lots of people being very critical of me at times, saying, 'You're hanging out' or 'You're not getting involved.' I used to reply, 'I didn't see the point of being involved in there when the ball was coming out the other side.' I would make a tackle and they would say, 'Well done, but you should be in the rucks.' Again, I would say, 'No, you should be where the ball is.' Fortunately, Gareth Jenkins, who was the Llanelli coach at the time, wanted me to play my own game. He could see the type of player I was.

*

I must have been doing something right because, after just four games in the seconds, I was selected for Ystradgynlais firsts.

*

There was another big change in my life at this time, which also cemented my decision to throw my lot in with Ystradgynlais, and that centred around a change of career. Alana and I were starting to get a little bit serious in our courting and were talking of getting married and planning our future. On hearing this Alana's father, who was an overman at Treforgan Colliery, took me aside for a chat.

He said, 'Look, we're opening a new pit in Treforgan near Crynant and there's going to be work for 50-odd years. I will get you a job and you will have security.' I had been working at a factory in Pontardawe at the time, and while I was doing well – I had just finished my training and was running a press shop and in charge of the night shift at the age of 22 – there was always the threat of redundancies in factories in the late '70s. I jumped at the chance; after all, it was a job with security and also a job which most of the other Ystrad rugby boys also did.

So, not only did I have to explain to my parents that I was going to play rugby, I also had to break it to them that I was going to work in a coal mine – they were horrified. They tried everything to get me to change my mind, but it was something that I felt was the right thing for me to do.

CHAPTER 2

Learning my Trade

YSTRADGYNLAIS PLAYED IN Section A of the West Wales League when I joined them in 1977, and to say that it was a personal baptism of fire would not be an overstatement. It was a tough, tough league packed with highly competitive and combative teams such as Kidwelly, Tumble, Vardre, Hendy and Pontarddulais.

The standard was really high and there were some great players who had just come out of first-class clubs like Llanelli, Neath and Swansea, not to mention the scrappers – uncompromising, don't-give-an-inch players – the huge percentage of whom were either steel workers or colliers, and there's no doubt they added a physical edge to an already tough game. The side which could intimidate the most was the most successful side. But you always put a performance in and they would respect you for it.

To be honest, it was a bit of a shock to me how violent it could get. Even in my first-class days there was so much going on – half the teams would be off the field with today's refereeing standards! There was unacceptable rucking and punching, and who knows what would be happening. The idea was: do not get caught. The referee then was the only adjudicator on the field; there were no assistant referees or TMOs. Each team would supply a touch judge to run the line, but they were so corrupt it was laughable. At Ystrad we had John CD running the line. On one occasion our wing ran around him and he still didn't put his flag up!

I was never a scrapper but I cannot say I didn't enjoy it, on a few occasions, when a punch-up happened. I wouldn't call it thuggery; I used the term 'controlled violence'. It was usually in the forwards but not always. Nine times out of ten no one was hurt apart from a few black eyes. No one ever seemed to get seriously injured and you would never wilfully try to really hurt somebody or maim them. In a way, the violence pulled a team together. There was camaraderie; if your mates were in there you were in there. That was really what built your team. It pulled you closer together – one in, all in. Willie John McBride established that with the 1974 Lions in South Africa with his '99' call.

The GP at our local health centre, Keith Hughes, an ex-Welsh international who also played for Llanelli, was not always sympathetic and once stitched me up without any local anaesthetic. Having said that, he also stitched up a really badly gashed eye needing 17 stitches and did a more sympathetic job. You have to look closely to see the scar.

During the same game my brother-in-law was also injured, but there was a night out planned as the wives were away in London. It was to be a team building outing so the injury had to wait! Unable to go to work on Monday, I received a call from Kevin asking me to take him to A&E at Morriston Hospital. Sitting in the waiting room a nurse saw my eye and called me in to see the doctor. I answered her by saying, 'It's not me, it's him!' After being examined Kevin had to have surgery on a fractured cheekbone, which caused him a lot of discomfort but not enough to interfere with Saturday's night out!

The game has progressed considerably since then. The first thing rugby had to do, as it was growing, was to clean its act up. As teams wanted to improve, they introduced video analysis of games and coaches began to get far more technical, and this led to identifying most of the dirty play that was going on. It soon became apparent that if you did do something you would be found out. But it did not change overnight; you still had your tough boys.

I would say that cracking down on the violence has been a good thing because we need to attract youngsters to the game. Junior rugby has become a massive part of the Welsh Rugby Union's promotion of the game, and mothers weren't going to allow their children to play a game that was dirty.

But back then, being punched or raked and needing stitches after being caught in a ruck was part and parcel of the game. You would wake up all battered and bruised on a Sunday morning and you would be off down to the club.

My father-in-law once told me, 'A man's hours are Friday night and Sunday mornings.' Saturdays consisted of playing a game of rugby and then taking your wife out. He would say, 'Sunday morning, down the club for surgery.' It was like a doctor's surgery but the main talking point was about the game the previous day. Everybody would come in and have their point of view. Some of the boys would have gone to watch Neath or Swansea – they were the two best supported first-class clubs, never Llanelli until I went there. You had four or five pints and then it was home for Sunday dinner, and a sleep in the afternoon.

*

The social side of the game was important, and for many it was one of the reasons they played rugby. It was a real family occasion with the wives and girlfriends being part of the ladies' supporters who cheered on the team during the game and organised the food afterwards. It suited me down to the ground and I realised I had made the right decision – the rugby club was at the heart of the town and had a lot more going for it than football ever did.

We would have great trips away and sing-songs in the clubhouse after games which our opponents would join in with. My first meeting with Alan Lewis, who went on to become the Llanelli backs coach, was in Pontarddulais where he was head coach at the time. They used to bring a choir with them; it was such a brilliant atmosphere. The camaraderie, the whole social side of it was hugely appealing. I now have friends for life. Notwithstanding local derby games, where the dislike was quite intense and certainly spilled into big punch-ups, we would regularly get large crowds for home games. But when we played a derby, especially against Abercrave or Ystalyfera, who were a few divisions beneath us and always saw us as a prized scalp, you could get upward of 500 people watching. They had all come to watch the fight!

When Ystrad decided, as a money-making opportunity for an end-of-season tour, to make it compulsory to wear bowler hats on a Saturday, it brought much amusement to the Abercrave players and supporters who referred to Ystrad in song as, 'Who are the twats in the bowler hats? Ystrad!' We also had a few songs about Abercrave! There were players, over the years, who transferred from Abercrave to Ystrad and were probably taken off the Christmas card list for doing so.

*

I had no idea that rugby would suit me as much as it did and I surprised everyone around me. I soon started making a name for myself and local journalists would come along and do write-ups in the local paper. That began to create interest and then, in 1978, I got selected to play for Brecknockshire County as a Number 8. It was my first taste of representative rugby and a real honour to be picked for your county. I went on to play for them 25 times and was awarded my county cap, which is on display next to my Wales cap in my house.

You were playing with boys from all around, including the
Neath prop Jeremy Pugh, the Builth Wells bully! He was really
committed to Brecknockshire as a county and I ended up in
the front row with him and we went on to tour New Zealand
together in 1988.

*

My first season with Ystradgynlais ended in disappointment
when I broke my arm playing against Vardre in the semi-final
of the Swansea Valley Cup. We always seemed to play against
Vardre in the semi-final or final, and they were always a tough
bunch.

It was probably the biggest game of my fledgling rugby
career at the time. On that particular occasion, I was caught
up in a collapsed maul and my arm snapped. It is a sickening
feeling because you know you are going to be sidelined for a
while. Fortunately, employers accepted it. You lost money but
not your job, and they were supportive of you playing sport.
Also, American Insurance helped!

That was a good thing, as there was absolutely no money
in the club game at that level. In fact, we made it to the final,
which we won, and I was in the club after the game and one
of the committeemen was handing out beer tickets. I was
sitting with the players, with my arm in plaster, and when he
came to me, he said, 'You didn't play,' and I didn't get any.
That is how it was – you had to be in the team to get your
two pints.

*

I was back in time for the following season and was able to
play my part in one of the most memorable games in the club's
history – against Llanelli in the Schweppes Cup.

It was my first taste of playing against a first-class side, packed with household names, and it is still talked about today. The whole village was there, it was all everyone talked about from the moment the draw was made to long after the final whistle. We had beaten Mountain Ash to make the next round of the draw and had all gathered around the television in the club on the Sunday to see us being pulled out of the hat first, to play at home, and then Llanelli came out. It was great.

Llanelli were packed with internationals and British Lions. I lined up as Number 8 opposite Derek Quinnell who would go on to coach me when I played for Wales, which was quite bizarre.

I remember it being a bitterly cold day. There was doubt at one stage whether the game would go ahead because the pitch had a deep frost covering it in the morning. As it turned out, the weather and conditions were a great leveller – something I found out from the other perspective when I swapped the blue of Ystradgynlais for the scarlet of Llanelli and played against so-called minnows in the Cup. I knew how tough it was going to be; people were out here to do or die, and they would find energy from somewhere. It was their Cup final.

The game itself was nip and tuck. We scored a drop goal and a penalty and they scored a try and converted it. Back then a try was worth four points, so the final score was 6–6. We should have won really as one of our wings dropped the ball over the try line with seconds to go.

On the final whistle someone asked, 'What happens now?' 'We have to go to Stradey Park for a replay.' I must admit the thought of that filled me with dread because we had had our best day and they had had their worst. There was no way they would be so off-key on their own patch.

But then we were told that Llanelli were going through as they had scored the only try. By the time we had eight pints, we were all thinking that we should have gone through were it not for missed opportunities. The reality was, we had had our day in the Schweppes Cup. It was a great moment for the club and a huge part of its history.

*

I measured myself by my improvement after each season. I was new to the game, I had no idea at the start, and I had to learn the laws of the game. But I generally felt that I was a reader of the game and could see the game, which used to annoy a lot of the boys at the start. They would call me a bloody seagull and say, 'Why don't you put your head in.' I would reply, 'Why would I put my head in there when the ball is over there?' I always liked to score tries and was top try scorer with Ystradgynlais on a couple of occasions.

I think it was a surprise to everybody how quickly I grasped the game. I was starting to make a name for myself and teams were beginning to mark me more closely.

*

A few seasons later, in 1981, we drew Swansea at home in the Cup. The most memorable thing I remember from that day was that Clive Rowlands, the former Wales captain and coach who lived in neighbouring Upper Cwmtwrch, came down to give us a team talk before the game. I will never forget his words; it was so inspirational we would have run through a brick wall. Clive was exceptional.

I was the tallest player in the Ystradgynlais team at that point and so was moved up to second row. We did not win a lineout all day. I was marking Richard Moriarty, who I ended up going to the 1987 Rugby World Cup in New Zealand with. I don't think anybody would have thought that at the time!

We decided that, if any trouble were to start, we would all stick together. Our plan held firm when their tight-head went at our loose-head in an early scrum – what he did not account for was the fact that the whole eight of us piled in. That really unsettled Swansea and we ended up narrowly missing out by a solitary penalty. Again, it was a game that we could have won but to go down to one of the top sides in Wales, 0–3, was no mean feat.

The history of Ystradgynlais in the Welsh Cup is exceptional. It started with Cardiff and Gareth Edwards coming to the Welfare Ground in 1974. Ystrad lost 0–11 but didn't disgrace themselves. Then you had Llanelli and Swansea and then Ystrad went on to beat Newport in 1994. It was a major date on the calendar for a second-class team to be drawn against a first-class team.

*

I played my first game of first-class rugby in the 1981 season – for Neath! The club was going through a pretty tough time and were starting to look for new players from local clubs. They had obviously picked up on me from somewhere or other and invited me to play for them on permit away against Maesteg. The system used to be, if you were registered with a second-class club, you were allowed to play on permit for a first-class club up to six times in any one season. After that they had to sign you or just not pick you again.

Maesteg were a top side at that time and had an exceptional back row built around their Number 8, a player called John Thomas. They won the Merit Table trophy twice around that time, and were a tough, tough side, particularly at their Old Parish ground.

I played Number 8 and we lost but Roy John, a committeeman and a former Welsh international, came to speak to me after the game and said, 'If you want to make it in this game, you need to go up to the front row.'

I replied, 'There's not a chance in hell of that happening because that's where all the fighting starts!'

He was the first one to plant the seed of me playing prop, but at that time I had absolutely no intention of playing prop. At the same time other first-class teams approached me suggesting I might have a future at a higher level if I switched to prop.

Shortly after, the Neath coaches, Brian Thomas and Ron Waldron, called around my house to see me. They knocked on my door and said, 'We would like you to join Neath.'

Brian Thomas said, 'Let me look at your hands.'

I held them out and Waldron said, 'I heard that you are pretty good with your fists.'

'I don't know where you heard that from,' I said. 'I'm not someone who reacts to violence or goes out onto the field to intimidate.'

The conversation put me off joining Neath. I wasn't scared of fighting; I was just more of a ball player.

Not long after, I was playing for Ystradgynlais against Pontarddulais and, unbeknown to me, a couple of Llanelli scouts were at the game to run the rule over Bont's second row. They went back and told the Llanelli coach that the second row wasn't what they were looking for but there was a boy called Buchanan, playing Number 8, who had caught the eye and could probably make it if he switched to the front row.

The opportunity to play at a higher level convinced me that I had to change position. I decided to play loose-head rather than tight-head, because from the tight-head position you were pinned in the scrum. At least from the loose-head you were on the outside, so I deemed it to be far more difficult as a tight-head. Also, there was a big hurdle in my way, quite literally, if I wanted to play on the other side of the front row, as my brother-in-law Kevin, the club captain, was playing there at the time. There was no way I was going to replace him as he'd played over 500 games for the club. When I told him what I had in mind he looked me in the eye and said, 'You will never make a prop as long as you have a hole in your backside.'

I never did weights. You didn't have the gyms like you do today, and there was no emphasis on strength and conditioning during training sessions, but I was quite naturally strong. From a young age I was lifting bales of hay and then I went down the colliery. So I felt that I had the strength to switch but the technical side was a major hurdle.

*

The offer to play on permit came soon after and I played my first game for Llanelli against Abertillery. I had my head well and truly stuffed up my backside – I spent every scrum staring our second row, Derek Quinnell, in the face!

Ray Gravell, who was captain, kept coming over to ask me if I was alright.

In fairness, Dai Evans, a Carmarthen boy who was our hooker, never once complained.

The scrum aside, I caught two kick-offs, ran, passed, supported and scored two tries. After the game all the talk was, 'Who is this prop?' But I always said back then, 'Don't use the word prop because I have no idea what I'm doing.'

*

On a number of occasions Neath and Llanelli tried to get permits for me to play, but because it was not in before midnight on a Monday, the Ystradgynlais committee refused. I resented the hell out of them at the time but it probably did me good as it gave me more time to learn my trade.

Eventually I reached the maximum number of permit games with Llanelli and was a little bit stunned when they said that they wanted me to join the club as a prop. Initially I was excited, but then it dawned on me that I had no idea what I was doing as far as propping was concerned, and realised that I was going to get seriously hurt if I didn't learn my trade properly.

So, as flattered as I was by the offer, I told Llanelli that while I wanted to join them, I first needed to go back to Ystradgynlais and learn the position. Fortunately, the coach at the time, John MacLean, understood and gave his backing to the plan.

My decision to switch positions caused a little bit of negativity within the town with some saying, 'Why should Ystradgynlais move a player to prop only for him to go and play for Llanelli?' Remember, Neath and Swansea were the two well-supported first-class sides locally.

Fortunately, Ystradgynlais Rugby Club and the coaches supported me, and I set out on my journey of playing prop in west Wales.

*

In the first season or two I had some really hard times and realised I needed some help. I decided to go and see Alan Lewis – or Big Lew as he was known – to get some tips on the technical aspects of propping. He had played for the All Whites and so knew his way around the scrum.

I knocked on his door in Ystalyfera and he called me in. I said, 'Look Al, Llanelli are looking at me to go down there as a prop and I'm just looking for a bit of advice on my positioning.' Now Big Lew is a real character – he once made the team he was coaching bring their bicycles to pre-season training and took the seats off before sending them on a 20-mile ride, and another time he made them run up the local mountain, backwards! But he knew his stuff.

He stood up, placed his foot on his couch and kicked it to one side, put his foot on his chair and pushed it the other way to make room, and caught hold of me in a scrum position. He drove me back against the wall, lifted me off the floor, squeezed me so hard my ribs nearly popped and told me, 'Forget it. You're not tough enough!'

'I just wanted to know where I put my feet,' I replied. The episode only served to make me more determined to prove people wrong.

*

One of my early lessons came against Seven Sisters, in the neighbouring valley, who had a prop by the name of Alan Rice at tight-head, a hooker called Boris, and a loose-head by the name of Brian Howells (Patch) – all three were west Wales warriors. Alan Rice, to be fair, took pity on me and started giving me advice. 'Put your feet wider and further back,' he said.

Boris looked at him and said, 'Ricey, what are you doing? Don't tell him what to do. Kill the bastard!' People were very helpful in some places.

I remember one guy coming up to me years later and saying, 'I remember giving you a hammering in Waunarlwydd.'

I said, 'You're right. It was the first season I played prop.' Then I added, 'Where did you play after that?'

He was correct though. It took me quite a while to grasp how to survive in the front row. I was still learning when I went to Llanelli for my first season.

*

Towards the end of my fourth season we had a live scrummaging session in Ystradgynlais which saw me go head-to-head with my brother-in-law. Afterwards he looked at me and said, 'You will make it.' I had improved so much from my first time that I could now challenge him, and he was regarded as one of the best technical tight-heads in west Wales.

The following season I joined Llanelli. I was 26 years old and still had a lot of learning to do as it turned out.

CHAPTER 3

Becoming a Scarlet

WHETHER YOU BELIEVE in serendipity or not, there's no doubt that my first-class rugby career with Llanelli came about thanks to the arrival of two new, enthusiastic, ambitious and forward-thinking coaches – namely Alan Lewis and Gareth Jenkins.

Llanelli had changed their coaching regime at the start of the 1982/83 season and Alan Lewis, along with his forwards coach Gareth Jenkins, were tasked with building a new team around pace and flair. As a result they were looking for players who they felt could play in a certain way that matched their vision.

I must have had the potential to fit into their plans as I had a phone call in January 1983 to ask if I would play against Swansea on a Wednesday night down at St Helen's. I realised that this was my big chance – I wanted to make it and this was my opportunity.

It was a massive game – as were all local derbies between the Jacks and the Turks – and there was something like 17,000 people packed into the ground. Swansea were full of internationals and were unbeaten so far that season. I was up against a prop called Gareth John who was regarded as a future star, capable of reaching British Lions standard. The rest of the Swansea pack was full of legends such as Geoff Wheel, Maurice Colclough, big hard men.

I had a torrid time in the scrum. Gareth John said afterwards that I was like a bad penny – he kept throwing me out but I kept coming back. I just threw myself into every ruck and maul and supported every area of the game I could get myself into.

Geoff Wheel made a comment that Dai Jenkins, the Llanelli physio, ran on to the field to treat me more times than he himself had run out to play for Swansea! I didn't disagree with that, as I had put myself in all sorts of situations and received a bit of a battering from my own enthusiasm.

We beat Swansea that night. A young David Pickering, our openside flanker, was man of the match by a country mile and went on to play for Wales and captain them from that performance. To think of any international rugby was still way beyond me at that stage, but seeing it happen to people around me did open my eyes to the possibilities that could exist in that environment. It was an injection of enthusiasm.

After the game Llanelli asked me to sign for them. Gareth told me about his vision for building a team and how they felt that I could fit into it.

He said, 'You've got the potential but you have a lot of work to do.'

Personally, I did not really know if I was ready or not but it was one of those situations where I just had to go and try.

The Swansea supporters at Ystradgynlais Rugby Club tried their best to dissuade me saying, 'Those Turks never give players from the Swansea Valley a chance.'

Others told me I would have splinters in my backside, that they wouldn't play me, that I would spend all my time on the bench. Remember, you could only use two substitutes back then and only come on if another player was genuinely injured. I was bombarded with all the negatives around as to why I shouldn't go, but I refused to listen. I reasoned, if I'm on the bench all the time then it would mean that I was just not good enough and I could always come back to Ystrad. The only option was to go and try. I never wanted to be a 'what if?' man.

With my mind made up however, there was still a hurdle to overcome – Alana, who was now my wife! Gareth Jenkins had to persuade her to allow me to transfer as she would rather me play for Ystrad. She had no thoughts of me playing a higher standard of rugby for Llanelli. My father-in-law was there as well, having this argument that I wasn't ready for it, but Gareth said, 'He is ready. He just needs the opportunity.'

In the end they compromised and said that I could join for a year – 35 years later I am still there!

*

Gareth Jenkins was an absolute Llanelli legend who had been at the club since playing for the youth team and had made 260 appearances. As a flanker he played in the famous victory over the All Blacks in 1972 and had toured Japan with Wales and would, no doubt, have won many caps for Wales if it were not for a serious knee injury. Alan, whom I had first met when he was with Pontarddulais, was equally enthusiastic and visionary. Alan also played for Llanelli 73 times, and would have been destined for Welsh honours but suffered a nasty injury against Swansea.

The first thing they did was introduce high levels of fitness to the squad – teams had perhaps ignored that side of the game over the years. They said, 'Right, we have got to get fitter, stronger and play a style of rugby that blows the opposition away.'

It was the start of the era of conditioning coaches, and they brought in Peter Herbert who had appeared on the television programme *Superstars*. I think he held the world record for the number of dips performed and was what we would call a fitness fanatic. I was never his favourite – he always thought that I was holding something back, that I was never giving it my all. I looked at it as always trying to finish the training session rather than blowing a gasket and burning out!

Neath were in the same boat – the time was right to build a team and they were looking to bring in new players – and they brought in a fitness guru called Alan Roper who used to run them ragged up and down the surrounding hills.

It used to take me over an hour to travel down the Swansea Valley, across the River Loughor, through Pemberton and into Stradey. It was quite a commitment but there were some boys coming from Cardigan. You had to be committed to doing it. You had to want to do it.

I soon realised that fitness was more than just training with the club twice a week. You had to put the time in on your own as well – but I knew that I had pace. Fortunately, I had friends who liked running, Malcolm Hopkins, Dai Isaac and Steve James, who were good runners and in turn would come and get me whether I wanted to go or not. Fitness was never my favourite part of the game but I knew that I had to do it. We used to run along a disused railway line from Abercrave to Ystrad and they would push me and pace me. There is no doubt that helped me immensely.

Our pre-season training was at places like Denham Avenue, Cefn Sidan Country Park and Stradey Woods – always running up hills, always pushing each other on. You knew that if you wanted to have that opportunity you had to reach new standards – there was no more hiding in the bushes having a cigarette as used to be the case with some players!

On the playing front it was very much a case of the changing of the guard. The same thing happened to me at the end of my playing career – I understood that it was pointless keeping the old players around as it meant that the young players, who were the future, wouldn't get enough playing time. It is contrary to what happens today, where they want them all to be super fit but don't give them enough rugby – but that's an argument for later in the book.

I joined Llanelli when most of the stars, your Derek Quinnells and Ray Gravells, were coming to the end of their careers. In their place Phil Davies arrived as a young Number 8 from Seven Sisters, David Pickering arrived as an openside flanker, Alun Davies came in on the blind side and the likes of Jeremy Cooper and Anthony Griffiths competed for places in the back row.

In the front row, out went Charlie Thomas, Howard Thomas and John 'Coch' Williams and in came myself, while Laurance Delaney moved across to the tight-head. You couldn't wish for anyone better in the front row with you; he was tough because of the fact that he would always stay in there. I remember Brian Williams battering him down the Gnoll once and Laurance did not give an inch, he stuck in there. He was phenomenal in his commitment and fully deserved his caps when they came.

The first thing you would do pre-season was to look around the changing room to see which new props were there. The first chance you got, you would get them in the scrum and see how good they were. The first live scrums became very competitive and would sometimes erupt into punch-ups. You were always on your toes.

At hooker Ceri Townley joined us from Bridgend to compete against the highly mobile David Fox. Phil May and Russell Cornelius made up a formidable second row.

We were well served at half-back by Mark Douglas, and later Jonathan Griffiths at 9 and Gary Pearce who was a point scoring machine and later moved to rugby league.

The outside-backs included a lot of young home-grown players from west Wales – Martin Gravelle, Nigel Davies, Simon Davies, Carwyn Davies, Dai Nichols, Kevin Thomas and Peter Hopkins. We were later joined by another 'local boy', in the form of Jonathan Davies when he made the switch from Neath.

*

I would like to take a moment here to pay my own tribute to the late Ray Gravell – what a man! He was one of those who was totally committed to the club, a Llanelli man through and through. He was also the most passionate Welshman you could wish to meet. He had the most brilliant sense of humour and you loved playing in a team with him as he would do things nobody else could do. We were playing against Swansea and, while we were preparing for the game, all of a sudden Gravs kicked their changing room door open and shouted, 'Come on the Jacks!' There was uproar.

Pickering was giving a team talk once and he declared, 'We have got to get physical!' There was an Olivia Newton-John song out at the time by that name and Gravs started singing 'Let's get physical'. That didn't go down well with Dai Pick.

He was an extraordinary Welshman and Scarlet. I really got to know him well and I have nothing but admiration for him as a person, a rugby player, and a Welshman. He was one of the great characters of the game and it was a pleasure playing with him.

I will always remember where I was when Gareth Jenkins phoned me to say that Gravs had passed away. Alana and I had gone to Madrid for a weekend and we were sitting in a restaurant. It was a real hard moment.

Sadly, I have experienced three such moments where we have lost people who were gone earlier than they should have been – Gravs was one, and then there was Hefin Jenkins and Stuart Gallacher, two outstanding servants of the club on and off the field of play.

*

There was no official league or European competitions back then but that's not to say that the so-called friendly games weren't fiercely competitive – you also had the Schweppes Welsh Cup and, best of all, regular fixtures against touring international sides. There were also far more games. They complain about player burnout today but it was not uncommon to have 60 games in a season, with regular Saturday and Wednesday fixtures.

The fixture list was terrific, with games against the top teams across the border. At least once a month we would cross the Severn Bridge and head to London, the Midlands, or the West Country. Because of the early starts we used to call at the Leigh Delamere Service Station for breakfast, and pile as much on our plates as we could because the club was paying – it was in the days before I had even heard the word nutritionist!

Sometimes we would come home after the game, other times we would stay away in a nice hotel. We once played in Northampton and I was roomed with Phil Davies. We had been delayed in traffic, so we checked in quickly and just managed to get to the game in time. They were tough games but then it was time for a few beers – sometimes it would be more than a few!

I was with Phil May and had lost Phil Davies somewhere. When I got back to the hotel in the early hours, I realised that he had the room key. I wasn't totally sure which room I was in and I told the night staff that I was in 228 but had no key. They told me not to worry and called the night porter who had a master key.

We then went up to the room and he opened the door and started walking away. I went in, calling out 'Tulip!', Phil's nickname. I looked around and all I could see were several suits hanging up around the room. Then this guy, in pyjamas, jumped out of bed and raised his fists like a professional boxer. I put my hands up, palms first, and said, 'Hold on! It's a mistake!'

Fortunately, the night porter was still in the corridor and I stepped back out and called, 'There's somebody in my room!' He panicked. Meanwhile, the door slammed shut in my face. It turned out that my room was on a totally different level!

We went back down to the front desk and I discovered that I had come close to jumping into bed with the snooker player Eddie Charlton! The rumours that I had already stripped off weren't true!

There must have been a tournament going on because I recognised one of the snooker referees from the television down at breakfast the next day. When I told him the story he said I was bloody lucky, because Eddie has boxed for Australia and he could've knocked me out. I replied, 'Well that would've made the newspapers.'

*

My first foreign trip was when we went over by ferry to Dublin to play Leinster at Donnybrook. They had an all-Irish front five in Phil Orr, Harry Harbison, Des Fitzgerald, Jim Glennon and Willie Anderson. Although I became friendly with them all later in my career, that first occasion was far from amicable.

Our front row was me, Laurance, and a young inexperienced hooker on permit from Aberystwyth. If we didn't realise how difficult it would be, we were soon to be enlightened when we went down for the first scrum. The referee gave the mark, so we crunched down ready to engage and all I saw was the Leinster pack going a couple of metres back, ready to charge. They hit us so hard I nearly lost consciousness. My legs went, I saw stars in my eyes and felt pins and needles in my arms. I was nearly knocked out by the physicality of the collision. I had the smelling salts and a bit of treatment and turned to the other two and said, 'I can't take another hit like that.'

We decided that Laurance would lead in and would come around with a sweep and, by the time they tried to engage,

I would come round at the last moment so they couldn't get a big hit on. Our tactic was ball in and ball away, because I was still in my naivety of scrummaging and still learning the game.

We eventually lost but it was a real nip and tuck game. While we were having a pint in the clubhouse after the game, Des Fitzgerald walked in and looked at me. He said, 'Aye. There you are.' I felt quite chuffed that he had recognised me. But then he said, 'I saw you for the first scrum but didn't see you again for the rest of the game.'

I replied, 'I don't think I would have finished the game if I had to take another scrum like that!' They were deeply passionate about that physical challenge.

I went out around Dublin with them afterwards for a few beers, and they wouldn't let me put my hand in my pocket. They were very hospitable and showed us a wonderful time.

When we played against London Welsh at Old Deer Park there would be thousands of Welsh exiles there, and afterwards there would be a choir in the clubhouse. It was always an enjoyable after-match atmosphere. Later we would go to the Orange Tree where we would meet up with players and supporters for a couple more beers! Playing against Harlequins at Twickenham was also an exceptional experience and very civilised rugby. I always remember the green of the changing rooms and the row of baths (the type we would have at home) where you could have a welcome soak after a hard game. Then I would end up going to Cross Keys on a wet and windy Wednesday night and get absolutely mullered.

Not all the English clubs were so genteel however, and when you went to Gloucester, Bath and Bristol, it was more like Welsh rugby.

My first visit to Bath was marred by an enthusiastic mistake. We kicked off and the ball went towards their wing, David Trick, who was a Commonwealth Games sprinter. Off I went. He was there for his pace and, not being the most natural of ball players, he was caught in two minds between kicking the ball or running.

We used to play for the rag doll, which was always hung from the crossbar, and there were thousands of people there watching me bearing down on Trick. I got within a yard, when he decided to kick. I arrived and absolutely flattened him as I was committed to the tackle. I hadn't done anything dirty – I wasn't penalised – and I got up thinking, 'I got him!' I turned around to see the whole Bath pack thundering towards me. They were a tough group of internationals – the likes of Nigel Redman and Gareth Chilcott – and they battered me! It made me realise that this wasn't going to be soft and all shaking hands!

*

Although I had undergone an apprenticeship of sorts playing prop in west Wales, I soon realised that I had a whole new level to climb with almost every fixture throwing me up against international tight-heads. It was a rude awakening but the challenge and the fixture list made me determined to stay in the team.

I was coming up against formidable props who were technically better than me or they were stronger than me. What I had to do was learn how to survive first. I was fortunate in that our hookers, Kerry Townley and David Fox, could hook a ball when my nose was almost touching the floor.

The ethos of the club was, without doubt, to play an expansive game of rugby and move the ball quickly, which suited me because I didn't want to be long in that scrum. If I had gone to a more forward orientated club I may not have had those opportunities.

On a personal level it was the challenge of going to Newport where you had Colin Smart, Spikey Watkins and Rhys Morgan, a formidable front row; then going up to Pontypool Park and the famous Pontypool front row with Graham Price, who was a gent of a man off the pitch, Bobby Windsor and Charlie Faulkner, not forgetting Staff Jones and Steve Jones and the likes of John Perkins backing them up. Then you would drop down to Cardiff and they had Jeff Whitefoot, Ian Eidman and Alan Phillips; in Bridgend there was Meredydd James, Ian Stephens and Jeff Davies – everywhere you went there were either British Lions or Welsh internationals.

And it didn't get any easier when we played the English sides who were equally blessed with the likes of Gary Pearce at Northampton, Austin Sheppard at Bristol and Gareth Chilcott at Bath. There were a lot of strong props around.

The toughest opponent I came up against in the scrum was the Scottish tight-head Ian Milne, who was with Harlequins. I will never forget the first time I played against him. We were shunted in the scrums and Phil May told me to do something with him. But he just got hold of me, like a vice, and every time I tried something he just tightened his hold on me.

At one stage I thought that I was going to pass out. The idea is that the tight-head puts himself in a situation where he lowers your neck position so that your airway constricts – it's physical and you're struggling to breathe, it can get quite frightening sometimes. You're trying to get a breath, you're trying to push and you're trying to scrummage. You soon learn not to get your neck in that kind of position. You move them around off your shoulder – that comes with experience.

In my early days I was barely hanging in there. But I was learning all the time and realised that if I changed my head position and adjusted my feet in a certain way, it made a big difference. In fairness to Llanelli, they put their faith in me and brought people in to coach me such as the British and Irish Lions legend Fran Cotton. He looked at me and said, 'You're scrummaging with your neck and your back. If you can get away with it, keep it going.' But he encouraged me to drop my legs a little bit lower. I had to learn how to bring my knee up and lock myself into the scrum.

It was tough. Alana used to run a bath for me after games and I would come home and not be able to then go down to the Ystrad club because I was in bits. I was aching in parts that I never knew that I had. I was in a lot of pain that first season and a half, and on several occasions Alana said to me, 'Give it up.' The thought never once crossed my mind.

*

Despite her initial reticence, Alana was incredibly supportive. It grew on you. People started to recognise me and I was beginning to make a name for myself in first-class rugby. My first season was really about surviving. But I started to show potential, and the more potential I showed the more games they gave me – the danger being that this can give you a false sense of understanding of where you are.

CHAPTER 4

Life Underground

AT THE SAME time as I was learning my trade as a prop forward, I was getting to grips with another trade surrounded by props of a different kind – ones that held the roof up!

I spent 15 years in all working underground and they were most probably the happiest of my working life. While the role of a collier can often be dangerous due to working in a tough environment, the camaraderie amongst the boys was something special and, much like rugby, you met great characters and made friends for life.

All this however was far from my mind during my first few weeks of acclimatising to life below ground. Having taken my father-in-law up on his offer of a job, I went to work at Treforgan Drift Mine in Crynant, a short three-mile journey over the mountain into the next valley.

I had asked myself if this was the life I wanted to buy into. The security was there, and I had decided that it was what I wanted. However, I can honestly say that during my first six months working underground, I thought I had made a major mistake. It was such a different environment, tough and harsh. I even toyed with the idea of trying to get my old job back in the factory.

Just changing from clean to dirty clothes to start your shift was a bloody job. You would get up and travel to work in the morning, walk into the baths' clean area, take off your clean clothes and then cross over to the dirty side and put your dirty work clothes on – it was soul-destroying at times. I will always remember the smell of the disinfectant used to wash the baths out hanging around like a bad taste in the mouth, and the stink of the dirty clothes speaks for itself. I used to take my work clothes home every Friday for a good wash, but I'm not sure everyone did that. You would be forgiven for thinking something had died in some lockers!

You had to get your timing right when it came to changing, as the spake – the open carriage which carried the colliers down the slope into the mine six at a time – would drop at 7am on the dot. You were in at 6.30am and had to change, get your orders and pick up whatever you needed, get on the spake and bang, down you would go. If they had to run a second spake for you they could dock your times.

Then, once you were down there, the air was damp and it was freezing cold, particularly in winter, with coal dust flying around. The air underground was circulated by huge fans so that there was clean air going down through the intake and dirty air coming back on the return. Fans were a big part of the safety aspect, ensuring that the mine was well ventilated. I once bumped into the manager, Mr Clarke, who said, 'The only ones working here are me and the fans!'

*

My first few days were spent being trained in self-rescue – what to do in certain scenarios – and I was told all about my safety equipment. Then you did three weeks training at Abernant Colliery, which was a deep mine situated in a valley above Pontardawe, doing basic jobs which were quite tedious, but it was all about getting you used to being in that environment.

I had a couple of options early on as the manager of Abernant Colliery was a big Llanelli supporter and wanted me to go there to work so he could look after me, but I decided upon the shorter journey over the mountain.

Treforgan was a drift mine which took the form of a tunnel built into the hillside sloping downwards, something that suited me just fine because I didn't want to go down a pit. I had been down Abernant in a cage and I just didn't feel comfortable. I always felt that working in a drift mine, if something went wrong, I could always attempt to walk out. That's not to say a drift mine didn't have its dangers. There was a major incident once when there was a runaway spake. My father-in-law was actually on it at the time and he told me quite a few men didn't go back underground after that experience.

Men lost their lives during my time underground, which was always tragic. It was always horrific when these things happened. When you reflect back, it was the type of industry where you knew you had to be ultra-careful and understand the risks involved. I had a few narrow misses but I think everyone did in one way or another. Sometimes you would be doing something that you knew you shouldn't have been doing, taking shortcuts. There were lots of accidents, people losing fingers, arms or eyes. It was tough but there was an almost acceptable level of danger. One, you were breathing in coal dust, and two, you were working in a huge hole in the ground. It was a really testing environment but you just got on with it.

There was an old side to Treforgan and a new side. The older drift was first sunk in the 1960s on the site of the even older Llwyn-Onn Colliery which was closed in 1927. The new drift had been opened in the late 1970s at the huge cost of around £7million. It was like a palace compared to the old one, a brand-new state-of-the-art enterprise with concrete slabs covering the arches supporting the roof and lighting everywhere – they had spent a fortune on it. It was my father-in-law's pride and joy. He used to call it God's Little Acre before moaning about those under his command saying, 'Pitch Wembley... team Cwmtwrch!'

He was quite a notorious overman and character. They

used to call him the Screaming Skull as you could always hear his voice barking out the orders. Work and rugby were his life. They used to say that there was more coal dust in the rugby club through him and the other colliers talking about work, than there was underground.

He knew that mine like the back of his hand. I was talking to him near the coalface on one occasion when he suddenly shouted, 'Stand back!' And the whole gable end just collapsed in. He knew that it was happening before it happened. He then sprang into action barking out orders, 'Get so and so down here!' and 'Get those chocks in!' They had to get it shored up as quickly as possible to get the coalface working again, because that's what made the money.

*

They chose the old drift mine to film a video to go with a Max Boyce song, showing Welsh outside-halves coming up from underground on the conveyor belt, which was quite an interesting reflection of what mining was to rugby at the time – although I think forwards were far more useful underground than half-backs!

Years later I played in Max's 'Golf Day' and he presented me with an award – for hitting the ball the shortest distance!

I got to know Max quite well, and when I was director of rugby development at the Scarlets we were interested in a couple of players from Glynneath. Max joked he would send people over the mountain to burn my house if we took any more of their team. He was very supportive of Welsh rugby in general, but Glynneath is his heart and soul.

*

When you undertake your training you are assigned to an experienced miner for your first few months. I was with Jack

Myers and Jerry Greenslade. Jack was chairman of Ystalyfera Rugby Club. Initially I spent my time down the old drift mine repairing roadways where the ground had come up. That often meant working in areas where the roof was only four-and-a-half feet high, so it was quite a task to find myself on my knees wading through water to arrive at the job and spend the day shovelling and digging. It was quite an experience – cold and damp with the water coming in.

Then they sent me to do my face training with a fireman appropriately called Mad Mike. I will never forget meeting him at the gate end. He handed me a shovel and said, 'Go and make a name for yourself.'

I had to crawl on my belly, through the chocks which supported the roof, to a certain part of the coalface where a machine was cutting the coal. The coal fell onto the conveyor belt which carried it out. You would have to move the chocks along as the machine cut deeper into the coal. There was only an 18-inch gap between the coal and the metal which prevented the coal from falling off the belt, and I had to get in with my shovel to keep cleaning in between the chocks so they could move them along. I hit everything – my head, my elbows. It was tough. There was dust flying around from the cutter. Then suddenly someone would come through, crawling on their bellies, and they would stop for a brief chat, always to do with this Saturday's game or last Saturday's.

It was scary down there but, fortunately, I only really spent significant time on the coalface during my training.

I even worked for a little while with a team known as the Commandos. The nickname was because they were a crack squad given the task of going down and moving the big machinery. They could move anything. Sometimes it was just a matter of getting the job done by hook or by crook, which could be quite risky at times.

Then an opportunity came up for me to work as a pump fitter – which was basically repairing the pumps which prevented the mine from becoming flooded. I was very fortunate in that, of the two boys who I shared that role with, one wanted to work nights regularly and the other afternoons. That left me with days regularly, which fitted in perfectly with my rugby as the shift ran from 7 o'clock in the morning to 2 o'clock in the afternoon. If I had gone on afternoon or night shift, that would have finished my opportunity to play rugby at a higher level because I wouldn't have been able to train properly.

*

It was a hard, physical environment but it toughened me up and played its part in helping with my rugby. As I have already said, I was never a gym monkey but the work made you strong. You would be given jobs such as going to salvage 18-inch pipes from the old drift. It would be a job which meant you could go home once it was done, so you would be running them down on your shoulder and chucking them about so you could get home earlier.

There were always challenges, everything was a test of strength. There were some really strong men working underground but I like to think that I held my own.

You would go into the blacksmith's shop and see how many times you could lift up the anvil inside a minute. We would also have what they called a cleft and sledge, where you would see who could break the bolt with the fewest number of hits. Gamesmanship came into it when they would hacksaw halfway through the bolt, and mask it with dirt!

The competitiveness could get a bit out of hand at times and nearly came to blows, but you soon realised you would get your cards if that happened.

*

Rugby was always a great topic of conversation, especially

when you went in on the Monday. If you had played against each other it could be quite hostile, especially if you had won!

I was walking down the new drift on my own once when I came across a group of Thyssen contractors taking a breather. One of them was Alan John, Barry John's brother and a former Llanelli player himself. He looked at me and said, 'I hear Llanelli want you to sign for them.'

I said, 'Well, it looks like I'm going to give it a go.' I was still with Ystradgynlais at the time.

As he started talking to me about the club, he opened up a tin which contained chewing tobacco, known as twist, soaked in rum. Twist, and also snuff, which the colliers used to stuff up their noses to stop the dust getting in, was widely used because when you travelled up the return, all the bad air hit you.

'Do you chew?' he asked me.

'No,' I replied.

'Do you fancy some?' The smell was quite enticing and so I accepted.

He handed me a piece and I placed it in my mouth, not realising that you shouldn't swallow it! I ended up being as sick as a dog. I will never forget him looking at me, no doubt thinking, 'You had better toughen up if you want to make it with the Scarlets.'

*

Despite the promise of 50 years of coal they closed Treforgan in 1985, having decided that it just wasn't viable, not cost effective. They had sunk millions of pounds into it – it was like a cathedral underground, everything was brand-new. From a safety point of view, life underground had come on a million miles. There was a lot of money invested in safety which, ironically, contributed to killing the industry in the end – the cost of providing a modern coalface was just too great. It meant that you had to dig more coal out. I think we ended up with coal being something like £24 a ton when you could buy it in from America or China for £18.

In the case of Treforgan, all the easy coal had been mined. The further you went in, the more geological problems you faced and the higher the cost, so you had to bring more coal out. Profit was the biggest stumbling block.

It was a really sad day when they closed that mine, as I said. The Treforgan days were my happiest – I had come to really enjoy working in that kind of environment. I would not have left there if it hadn't closed, I would have remained working there until it was time to retire and the rest of my life would have changed dramatically.

*

Once they had decided to mothball Treforgan, they moved people to different collieries and I ended up further down the Dulais Valley in Blaenant, which is home to Cefn Coed Mining Museum today.

I had to change my role as they already had people doing the job I was doing before. You basically went into a labouring environment because all the best jobs were already taken. I ended up working on the bakerfort, which was a sort of monorail – Treforgan was rail and timber – which took you down the drift. They had a drift and a pit at Blaenant.

I was just happy to have a job as Alana and I were now married. It was just the natural course of things. My brother-in-law, Kevin, was my best man and we had the reception at Ystradgynlais Rugby Club – where else?

The biggest problem with Blaenant was everyone was a Neath supporter! I was established in the Llanelli side by that time and everyone used to read the back pages of the newspapers, so there was a lot of banter flying around. The games between Neath and Llanelli were always nip and tuck. They had put a formidable side together and it was a bit like a war. They had Thorburn kicking penalties from everywhere and they had Brian Williams, Kevin Phillips and John Davies in the front row, and Gareth Llewellyn and Huw Richards in the second row.

Phil Pugh and Dai Morgan, the Neath back rowers, were already working at Blaenant when I arrived there, and the undermanager told me not to follow them!

'Don't turn out like Phil Pugh and Dai Morgan, whatever you do!'

They were both good boys, tough men and hard rugby players. In fairness, Phil never tried to wind me up at work – he wasn't that sort of bloke – but he would do you on the field if you ended up in the wrong place; just ask Rupert Moon! Although Rupert started out with Abertillery, he made a name for himself with Neath but then chose to come to Stradey Park. His first game back at the Gnoll was always going to be a challenge and, sure enough, Phil gave him quite the welcome – a picture appeared in the sports pages the following day showing the referee giving Phil the red card, and in the background poor Rupert is in a crumpled heap on the floor.

I always got on with Phil and Dai – I had even played alongside Dai for Ystrad. He was in the side the time we drew with Llanelli.

Dai was immensely strong and quick enough to have played on the wing. He could have gone a lot further than he did but I suppose rugby wasn't the be-all and end-all for him, he just enjoyed the social side of the game.

*

The colliery even had its own rugby team, made up mainly of Crynant, Ystrad and Seven Sisters boys. We used to play against different companies and collieries. We were quite successful. They were never short of players because if you played for the colliery team you'd be able to finish early for training or on match days. You'd get on the spake and the undermanager would come and check who was on board, as the boys were as wicked as hell and there would always be some on there who didn't even know what a rugby ball looked like!

There was one instance when Ronnie Star, who was quite a good wing in his time, was sat next to me and the undermanager said, 'Where are you going, Ronnie?'

'To play rugby, Mr Trailer,' he said.

'I will be checking on you,' he replied. Ronnie was in his 60s!

*

The friendships formed were immense. You would share your food with your colleagues – the only thing you wouldn't do is show someone else your pay slip! Money was a big driver in the industry – you would sometimes get a higher rate for certain tasks.

The characters, you couldn't make them up. We were at the coalface once and the fireman at the time, a guy from Banwen, had designed a new method of boring and firing to cut through rock, which he claimed would allow you to get more yards – you were paid by the yardage. He was explaining to me how it all worked: 'We'll drill in here, and drill in there, and put more powder in. We'll get more stone out and get more yardage.'

It's quite a sight to see, these boring machines in action – the noise is horrific.

They were just about ready to fire and he told me get in the manhole. He detonated, and all I can remember is toolboxes flying past where I was sheltered! The whole lot collapsed.

There was one hell of a mess. It had blown out all the arches and everything.

*

I have so many memories. We were playing Newport away once and the bus was leaving at 11am, so I went to see the engineer on the Friday and asked if I could finish an hour earlier the next day. 'Everyone knows I'm a Llanelli supporter,' he said. 'I will get so much grief. I'll tell you what, come in an hour early.' And so I had to go in at 4am, work underground until 11am, come out, catch the bus and go and play.

If you were working a double shift and you were injured, you just had to strap yourself up and go to work. You didn't want to lose a double time shift.

*

I used to have a red setter called Rusty who would come on my runs with me, which must have benefited him as he was a fine specimen and was sought-after for breeding. I was once offered the pick of the litter in return for loaning him out, and sold the pup to one of the boys, Terry, in the colliery.

Terry was such a character and loved that dog so much that he decided to bring it into work to show the boys. The manager caught sight of him.

'What on earth have you got on the end of that lead?' he demanded.

Terry looked at him and replied, 'It's a dog, Mr Clarke.'

'I was talking to the dog.' That sums up miners' humour to me in a nutshell.

*

My time underground coincided with one of the most tumultuous periods in the industry's history – the year-long 1984 miners' strike. The towns and villages of the south Wales Valleys were built on the back of coal, and the dispute shook the very heart of all those communities.

I was never political but I supported the National Union of Mineworkers and voted in favour of the strike – we all thought that it would be over in a month.

The NUM was a strong union, with good values and good people, but I did think that during meetings they would always find the biggest 'header' going, and ask them to say a few words! I used to think, 'Here we go.'

A lot of people faced a lot of hardship over the course of that year. Fortunately, the community was supportive and there were lots of food parcels for the boys and their families. I was lucky inasmuch as I did a bit of safety work – it wasn't frowned upon to help keep the mines in working order, as it would do neither side any good if they were flooded when we decided to go back – for which you got paid.

I was also lucky that Alana was teaching, so we had a regular income coming in. There was also a small silver lining in that we had bought an old house in Ystradgynlais and I was able to spend a lot of time renovating it during the strike.

Llanelli never offered to find me a job but I was never looking. As long as I was training and available for games it was fine. A lot of the boys were in demanding jobs at that time, the mines or steelworks.

*

The strike went on and on and, in the end, you didn't really know whether it was Arthur Scargill against Maggie Thatcher or Maggie Thatcher against Arthur Scargill – and the miners were caught in the middle. I think it became very personal between the pair of them.

I did go on a couple of protest marches up to Sheffield and I have never experienced anything like it. The noise was incredible; you had ranks of policemen banging their truncheons against their riot shields. I turned to my mate, Shem, and said, 'I think we're in the wrong place here at the wrong time.'

Arthur Scargill was hanging out of a window trying to address the crowd – it was quite a fiery moment filled with passion and anger. It was something that I had never experienced before, an intimidating time.

The police were pitched against the miners. It was horrible. But there were also moments of real hope that came out of it such as the food parcels and food kitchens – communities pulled together.

Llanelli were good to me, to be fair, although one of the committee, Peter Rees – who had played for Wales back in the day and was manager of the power station in Carmarthen, which of course relied upon coal – pulled me aside. He said, 'Now listen Anthony, you are playing for Llanelli now and we can't have pictures of you throwing stones at these coal lorries ending up in the newspapers.'

I replied, 'Peter, I'm the best stone thrower we've got!'

*

In all honesty, it was a fight that we were never going to win. The miners had previously been on strike in the late '70s, when their industrial action had caused power cuts and blackouts. Maggie Thatcher and the Conservative Government had learnt from this and had quietly stockpiled huge amounts of coal so that, when the strike came around in 1984, they had enough coal supplies to break the miners.

I knew that the miners were fighting for their livelihoods, but there was also that feeling that it was only a matter of time before the mining industry became obsolete. Fossil fuels were going to be phased out in Britain and I had already experienced Treforgan closing.

In the end we just went back to work and carried on. We were fortunate at Blaenant that there weren't many code-breakers who had broken the strike, sparing us the animosity and reprisals that blighted some pits.

*

One of the more depressing aspects to come out of the strike was the fact that it drove a wedge between the miners and the police.

Not long after the strike, I came home from work one day and Alana told me that two policemen, one with a flat cap and the other with a bobby's helmet, had called around asking to speak to me.

'Oh, right,' I said, 'I wonder what that's all about.' I was wracking my brain to remember if I had done anything untoward.

They returned later that evening and asked if they could speak to me. I invited them in and the one in the flat cap, who was obviously a high-ranking officer, said, 'Look Anthony, how would you feel about joining the police?' Confusion suddenly replaced any feelings of guilt!

'You would then be able to play for us,' he explained, and it all became clear – they were looking for a prop!

South Wales Police RFC at that time were basically a first-class club and played against the top sides on a regular basis. They had a great squad with the likes of Wales centre Bleddyn Bowen, Sean Legg, Steve Sutton, Colin Hillman, Hugh Williams-Jones and even Phil Davies had played for them for a while. Also, they were, to all intents and purposes, the first professional rugby team in the country when you take into account all the time their players were given away from duties to train and play.

Now I respect the police, but my answer was a firm 'no, thank you'. I really felt that I had settled into the mining industry and was enjoying it. I felt comfortable and wasn't looking for anything else. Also, I didn't want to swap, which would have been seen by many of my workmates as changing sides.

I tried to offset my decision by saying, 'I don't think I would pass the entrance exam.'

To which they replied, 'Can you write your name and address? That's all we're looking for.'

They must have really wanted me because, when I politely declined, they tried to get me to volunteer as a special constable so I would be able to play for them.

My answer to that was, 'What does that pay?'

'Not a lot but you get free boots.'

I replied, 'I don't think that's for me.'

CHAPTER 5

Cup Runs
and Touring Teams

I PLAYED MY club rugby in the time before the introduction of formal leagues. Although our so-called 'friendlies' were organised into the Whitbread Merit Table, it was based upon the percentage of wins you chalked up in a season and lacked the intensity of today's PRO14 and European Cup competitions. But, as mentioned, that's not to say we didn't have special occasions of our own in the form of the Welsh Cup and the visits of touring international teams. The latter stages of the Cup and fixtures against international sides always attracted sell-out crowds, which would see close to 11,000 people packed into Stradey Park, creating the kind of atmosphere the regions would be quite envious of today.

One of my biggest supporters was my father, who had decided that he had to go and buy a book on rugby to study the game when my career started taking off. He loved coming along to games but, unfortunately, when he was 40 he became unwell and was diagnosed as having a tumour on the brain. They didn't think that he was going to live, so they flew him by helicopter to a specialist centre in Oxford for treatment. They kept him awake and used lasers to cut into his brain. The result was his brain would slowly die away as he got older – like dementia – but it bought him extra time with us.

He had to stop driving, so my mother used to insist I go and pick him up for games. He used to love coming along and followed me right through my playing days. He would have complimentary tickets down at Stradey and people used to look out for him in the end and take him up to his seat in the stand. They'd say, 'Don't worry about your father, we'll look after him.' I would come up after the game and he'd be in the middle of everybody enjoying the company. He was a well-respected man in the area to be fair, and people still come up to me today to say what a gentleman he was.

My mother, on the other hand, only ever came to watch me play on one occasion, when we played against Fiji. She spent ten minutes watching the anthems and the kick-off; then, not long after, she was out to the car park – she couldn't stand it. I remember her telling me, 'It's violence.' That was the only game she ever watched me play.

I know I am biased but I believe we had the most passionate supporters going. People have often called Llanelli supporters 'one-eyed' but I have met plenty of Neath or Swansea supporters who are as equally one-eyed! Llanelli supporters are very loyal to the club, and they don't always necessarily live in the town. People would travel from all over to support Llanelli, especially for the big games.

Club rugby was 'tribal', and every supporter supported town and village teams with loyalty, having a sense of belonging where players and supporters mixed after games. Win or lose, you would run the gauntlet of the Patrons' bar at Stradey Park or the Neath clubhouse or the club at St Helen's, where supporters would be able to voice their opinions, sometimes good and sometimes bad. They shared in the success and failures of the team, and maybe we haven't been able to recapture this with the regions as yet. It's something we need to work on. You also have to remember that pre-regional club rugby, the amateur game, was always a 3 o'clock kick-off on a Saturday and everyone could set their day out. Saturday afternoon was always 'rugby time', along with 7 o'clock on a Wednesday night.

*

Games against touring teams in particular were always highly anticipated by players and supporters alike. It's a tradition that has been sadly lost to the game with the advent of professionalism and greater demands upon players' time. The big southern hemisphere sides used to embark on regular Grand Slam tours of Great Britain and Ireland, facing all four home nations over a couple of months or so whilst playing against a handful of select club sides in between.

Fortunately, Llanelli were almost always chosen to play against the touring teams, and they were fantastic occasions for the club – it was the equivalent of junior clubs playing against first-class teams in the Cup.

My first game against a touring international side came against Australia in November 1984, my first season proper playing for Llanelli. The 1984 Wallabies, coached by Alan Jones and packed with stars such as Nick Farr-Jones, Michael Lynagh, David Campese and the ridiculously talented Mark Ella, were probably the top side in the world at the time. They were the first and only Australian side to achieve a Grand Slam, beating all the home nations.

It was a midweek game, on the Tuesday afternoon before they played against Wales in Cardiff. So they were depleted, but they were still a side packed with experienced international players. And we were not at full strength either as Phil Lewis, Alun Davies and David Pickering were all rested having been selected for Wales on the Saturday, and Phil May was unavailable.

The build-up and excitement around the game was tremendous, and was far different to your usual home game. It was a special occasion. We had to meet at the clubhouse by 11am, and were taken down to the Ashburnham Hotel in Pembrey for a pre-match lunch. The real purpose was to bring us together collectively and to focus our minds – it was where the side who famously beat the 1972 All Blacks went and the routine became a tradition with Llanelli.

The club has always been able to make a big occasion special, and although it was a Tuesday afternoon kick-off, Llanelli was alive, it was a full house. It was an incredible feeling arriving at Stradey Park. It seemed that everyone in west Wales had taken the day off and was coming to watch the game.

The crowd on the walk-up was massive and really a sight to see. It was like looking at Wembley Way. Denham Avenue, the road leading to the ground, was a mass of people. They had parked their cars wherever they could and then walked to Stradey Park. It sent shivers down your spine. It was part of the psychology from the coaches – they wanted us to arrive through the crowd so it emphasised the occasion and what it meant to the supporters.

It was extra special for me as it was my first such occasion and I had a spring in my step running out of the players' tunnel into a wall of noise – the Regimental Band of the Welsh Guards and a choir were on the pitch warming the crowd up and building a great atmosphere.

I don't think many people gave us a chance but, the important thing was, we believed that we could do something and we knew the result was going to be special if we could win.

It was a tough, rugged uncompromising game – a level above your normal club game – but we were psyched-up and in the right frame of mind for the challenge. The more we realised that we were in the game, the more our confidence grew, and thanks to tries from our wing, Edward Ellis, and openside flanker, Jeremy Cooper, we ran out 19–16 winners.

The result has never really been properly recognised as it

fell in the shadow of the 1972 win over the All Blacks and certainly the win over the World Champion Wallabies in 1992, as that was a full-strength Test team. But, nevertheless, it was a victory against a touring international side.

I don't remember too much about after the game, other than I had to leave for home quite early because, being a week night, I had to be up at 6am for work the next morning! That was the reality of playing rugby in the amateur days – your day job took priority.

*

My next club game against an international side came around the following year, 1985, this time against the free-flowing Fijians. They were flamboyant rugby players and they could certainly play with ball in hand. It was another big occasion down a packed Stradey Park.

Once again it was a Tuesday afternoon fixture, taking place on 5 November and, fittingly for bonfire night, it was a cracker of a game although our performance in the first half was more of a damp squib. We made the mistake of trying to play Fiji at their own game and were far too loose. The Fijians pounced on our errors, scored three tries in 12 minutes and raced into a 25-point lead – once they received the ball, they were gone.

Half-time was fast approaching and it was going to be a massive embarrassment to us if we didn't do something about it. Although I was not the captain, I felt compelled to say something on that occasion. We were gathered behind the posts, waiting for a conversion attempt following the Fijians' third try, and I gave my opinion – I said a few home truths. I just felt things needed to be said. Dai Fox said afterwards that we needed that.

We hadn't really turned up until that point. The first thing we had to do was to be far more competitive in the contact area and deny them quick possession. We had fallen into the trap of playing a game that suited Fiji far more than it suited us.

We became focused and got on top up-front. We went direct, straight down the middle, and we started to play – everyone stepped up. Once we scored our first try, our momentum kept building and they couldn't cope with it.

Our change of tactics was reflected by the fact that all three of the tries we scored were scored by forwards, including one from yours truly.

As well as our pack played, our half-backs, Jonathan Griffiths and Gary Pearce – who scored his customary drop goal – took over the control of the game superbly.

The score at the final whistle was 31–28. I believe it was one of the greatest comebacks in the history of Llanelli Rugby Football Club – to win a game against an international team in such a manner. It was a terrific result.

After the game we all went to the Stradey Park Hotel where Fiji were staying for the post-match dinner. I had kept my Llanelli jersey after the game against Australia because it was such a special occasion to play against a touring side for the first time. But when the Fijian manager asked if I wanted to swap, I agreed. He invited me to a room to collect his side's jersey and I followed him upstairs. On opening the door I saw that all the furniture had been moved out of the room, and the Fijian players and management were all sitting crossed-legged on the floor around this big bowl. One of the players had a guitar and they were all singing along. It was a fantastic atmosphere.

I noticed they were all drinking what looked like muddy water out of that bowl in the middle – it was a drink called kava, made from a plant found in the Pacific Islands.

They invited me to sit with them and gave me a cup of this kava – it was stronger than any alcohol I had ever drunk. I left that room with a Fijian jersey and quite a head on! I didn't feel right.

That was the start of my relationship with Fiji which would see me go on to tour the country and even play for the Fijian Barbarians. The invitation to play, in a game against Bath, followed on from me being named man of the match in the Stradey game. It was a real honour and, I like to think, a big endorsement of my open style of play to have been asked. I obviously accepted, and ran out on the Recreation Ground to face the likes of Nigel Redman and Gareth Chilcott. I will never forget the look on Chilcott's face when he saw me.

'What the hell are you doing here?!' he asked.

'Helping out,' was all I could reply.

Now my new teammates were a little bit loose with their feet, if you know what I mean. At one point Chilcott turned to me and said, 'For goodness sake Buck, have a word with them! They are putting their feet all over the place.' They were ferocious ruckers of the ball to be fair.

I replied, 'Hey, they are stamping on me as well.' They had no idea who the white legs at the bottom of rucks belonged to!

It was a great occasion to be part of and I enjoyed the post-match function but had learned my lesson and left the kava well alone!

*

There is a special romanticism surrounding the visit of New Zealand to Llanelli, born out of the famous 9–3 victory in 1972 in the days of legendary Scarlets such as Phil Bennett, Ray Gravell, Delme Thomas and Derek Quinnell. When you remember that the pubs had been drunk dry in 1972 – as mentioned in the Max Boyce song – it brought it home to you what it meant to the supporters.

I was presented with the opportunity of joining that

exclusive club when a full-strength New Zealand side arrived for a Saturday fixture in November 1989, but we saw our chances, quite literally, blown away.

Wayne Shelford's World Cup winning All Blacks arrived at Stradey Park at the same time as one of the worst storms west Wales had seen in decades – it was a real typhoon. I had never seen anything like it, the wind and rain, it was horrific. Without doubt, they were the worst conditions I ever played in. I believe that if it had been any side other than New Zealand, the game would never have been played. The only saving grace was there was not much surface water on the pitch – Stradey was always kept in tip-top condition and was a great surface to play on.

We met early and went to the Ashburnham for the pre-match meal once more. I will never forget looking out the window and seeing the golf flag on the green bent over double by the wind. I thought, 'There's no way that this game will be on.' But the message came, 'The game is on. They want to play.'

The weather was so bad that they had to close a temporary stand which had been erected on the Tanner Bank. But the crowd still turned out. It was a massive occasion which everyone had built up, and then this storm came along.

'Buck' Shelford was captain alongside the likes of Sean Fitzpatrick, Steve McDowall, Gary Whetton and Zinzan Brooke in the pack, while Grant Fox, Joe Stanley, Walter Little and Craig Innes lit up the backs. What a team! But we went into that game believing that we had a chance. By then we had become an experienced team, full of internationals. We were no longer a developing side, we were a quality side going to play against the best team in the world. Gareth Jenkins was one of the stars of the 1972 game and now, as coach, was drumming it into us what it would mean to our supporters if we could win again and how we would become absolute legends amongst the Stradey faithful.

This was my second occasion of facing the All Black haka. I have been asked on many occasions what it is like, and there is no doubt they gain a huge advantage and momentum by doing it. It has, however, been one of the memories that I will cherish in my rugby career, and even to this day I love to watch the haka before every game they play.

The wind was howling straight down the pitch towards the town end, coming up from Kidwelly, and as a result the lineouts were a total shambles. I think every one of them ended up with a scrum for the ball being not straight. It was impossible to throw it in.

I lost count of how many scrums there were but there were a hell of a lot of them because of the conditions. The ball wasn't just like a bar of soap; you sometimes manage to hold on to a bar of soap!

The front row on the day was myself, Laurance on the tight-head and a 19 year old from Beddau, by the name of Andrew Lamerton, as hooker who would soon go on to play for Wales. I was up against Richard Lowe, with Sean Fitzpatrick and Steve McDowall who were a World Cup winning front row, but I like to think that we more than held our own.

We played into the wind first half and were only losing 0–7 at half-time – we were in the game. With the wind in our favour for the second half, we turned around thinking this was going to be another memorable occasion down at Stradey.

What we didn't foresee, though, was one of the finest displays from a fly-half on how to control a game when playing into the wind. We had never seen anything like it before. Instead of kicking-off from the middle of the field, Grant Fox went and stood amongst his forwards, drop-kicked the ball, and the forwards remained where they were but, as the wind was so strong, the ball came back to them.

They basically starved us of all possession and never gave us a sniff of points. They never allowed us to gain any momentum, even when we had the wind in our favour. I give them credit for that. If we had got a foothold in the game, I think we could have done something. Looking back, we missed an opportunity to go down in history.

When we had wind advantage, we thought that we had them where we wanted them. At half-time we said, 'Get a score and we can take this game.' But you have to take your hats off to them for their second-half display – they added another try and ran out 0–11 winners.

They were world champions. They played a game that you have to sit back and admire, they were a fantastic team. They have had so many brilliant sides, but this one was probably their best ever.

The next time they came over, I was team manager and they put 80-odd points on us.

*

When it comes to the WRU Challenge Cup – or the Schweppes Cup as it used to be known due to its sponsors – Llanelli RFC are the undisputed Cup kings.

Llanelli played in the first-ever Welsh Challenge Cup final in 1972, losing out narrowly, 15–9, to Neath and have gone on to win it 14 times over the years and been runners-up six times. My personal involvement is I played in three Cup finals with Llanelli, picking up two winners' medals in the process.

I remember one Cup game in particular at Stradey, against the great Pontypool, or 'Pooler' as their supporters would chant. They came to Stradey full of internationals. I will never forget it was one of those times when the Pontypool supporters really made their voices heard at Stradey with the chant of 'Pooler Pooler'.

I was still learning my trade as a loose-head prop and I was up against one of the greatest tight-heads of the time,

Graham Price. We had a scrum on our 22 where we used a Channel 1 ball which allowed Jonathan Griffiths to box kick into the goal area. I decided to leave the scrum through the side door, running around, catching the ball and scoring a try under the posts. (With the game being drawn at 15–15, this meant that we went through on a try count. This reflects back to my Ystradgynlais v Llanelli game where we had drawn 6–6 and they went through after scoring the only try.) I can assure you I never had an opportunity to try that again as Pricey just clamped me in there.

Whenever Phil Steel, who carries out a similar role for the BBC as Gravs did for S4C, gets the chance to put me in front of the camera alongside Graham Price, he always says, 'Tell us the story of that try, Bucks.'

*

Cup games, traditionally, were something everyone in Wales would look forward to, especially when it came to the final. We all threw everything we had into those games. You had earned the right to be in the final, you had got there by coming through some close, hard-fought games. The team always prepared itself for the Cup and had the mentality to win. Lots of people have asked me what the secret of Llanelli's winning streak is – all I can say is success breeds success and we all knew the club's history in the Cup and we carried that tradition on our shoulders.

My first visit to the Arms Park for a final came against Cardiff in 1985, and there was nothing like it. It was always the final game of the season and the supporters treated it with a carnival atmosphere in the May sunshine. I have played for my country in big games but playing for your club side on such occasions is really special because you are playing alongside your mates.

Getting on the bus with your teammates, the team talk

and preparation, arriving at the stadium and going inside and seeing the changing rooms with the big bath – it was just an incredible occasion.

We met up at Terry Griffiths' snooker hall – everyone had to set off from Llanelli together on the team bus (if you needed they would put you up in a hotel in the town the night before).

What an occasion it was. You travelled along the M4 and all the buses, packed with Llanelli supporters going towards Cardiff, took your breath away and filled you with excitement. Someone had hung a sign on one of the bridges saying, 'Would the last person out of Llanelli switch the lights off!'

As for the game, Jonathan Griffiths opened the scoring for us with a well worked try, but scores from Alan Phillips and Gerald Cordell put Cardiff ahead. We were behind for most of the game and were trailing 14–12 when Gary Pearce produced his trademark drop goal deep in injury time to win the game. It was a real nail-biter, especially as Gareth Davies fired a drop goal narrowly wide of our posts minutes later with the last kick of the game.

We had won 14–15! It was special climbing up the steps into the stand to receive the Cup – I will never forget looking down on the thousands of Llanelli supporters who had invaded the pitch to gather below us.

The tradition after the game was that we stayed for a few drinks, but then it was always back on the bus to Stradey. There would be a sing-song on the bus and a massive cheer went up as we crossed the Loughor bridge which brought us back home to Llanelli.

There were quite a few good singers amongst the boys. I was never great at remembering words to songs, and whenever we went away we always had a good sing-song. The other thing was having a good drink, socialising with your teammates. I think it was the same with all Welsh sides at that time. It was part of the tradition and camaraderie of playing rugby. It was also important in the building of team spirit.

*

We were back at the Arms Park three seasons later for a Cup final against our arch rivals Neath, and we climbed those steps up into the stand to collect our winners' medals once again thanks in no small part to the performance of our new Number 10, Jonathan Davies.

There's no doubt that when you look back at the outside-halves who have graced Stradey Park – Barry John, Phil Bennett, Gareth Davies and Gary Pearce – Jonathan Davies was amongst the best. He was an exceptional player.

Building a great team is a bit like a jigsaw puzzle. You have to fit your players in and around the team, but you need your half-backs to be special. When you have someone like Jiffy playing 10, you know you are going forwards and the game is going to be played with a lot of width. You were always confident when he was in the side; you just knew that you were going to win the game.

It was quite a coup getting him from Neath – but he was a Gwendraeth Valley boy so Llanelli was always going to be his club.

Nevertheless, his move upset the Neath supporters and he took a bit of stick from the Gnoll faithful. He still talks about a letter he had from a Neath supporter on the morning of that Cup final – I don't know what was in it but it didn't say nice things.

Jiffy had the last laugh though as he pulled the strings superbly in a man-of-the-match performance. We just took it by storm. We started off like an express train and scored quite early and the game went away from Neath very quickly and we won 28–13. Ieuan Evans scored a brilliant try after following up his own kick ahead, before my old mate Laurance Delaney caught a wayward throw by their hooker, Kevin Phillips, near the back of a lineout on the Neath line, and gleefully dived over for a popular score. Gary Jones added a third following a scrum.

Once again, it was an amazing experience to play on such a stage as the Arms Park. The game broke the world record for a crowd watching a club game at the time – 56,000.

Paul Thorburn was taken off with concussion during the game which led to quite a funny situation the following day. A friend of mine, Kevin Williams, had broken his neck playing for Brecknockshire County and was in Neath General Hospital. I decided to take the Cup to the hospital to show him in an effort to cheer him up a little.

When I walked through the door I came face to face with Brian Thomas and Ron Waldron who were there to visit Paul Thorburn. You can imagine how well that went down!

Thomas looked at me and said, 'You're the last bastard we want to see!'

*

The following season saw a rematch as we both made it to the final again. Neath arrived intent on revenge, and having had an almost invincible season in which they set a new world record for the number of tries and points scored by a club side, they were the firm favourites.

We were without Jonathan, who had gone North by then. Although we were far from being a one-man team, any side in the world would have been weakened without him – just look at how Wales struggled to find another like Jonathan. Saying that, his replacement, a youngster by the name of Colin Stephens, would go on to be a great player.

The game also saw us face David Pickering, who had made the move across to the Gnoll that season. He was a Neath boy and I am sure, like Jonathan, he just wanted to play for his home team. He came back from a South Seas tour having had a nasty head injury against Fiji in 1986 which in reality he did well to recover from. He could also play a couple of positions, including scrum-half. He was a talented rugby player.

The game was certainly well anticipated, as a new world record was set when 58,000 supporters turned up!

Colin Stevens took a leaf out of Gary Pearce's book and opened the scoring with a drop goal early on, but their aggressive Number 8, Mark Jones, stormed over for a try not long after that to take the lead. We regained the advantage with a penalty but in the second half Brian Williams, their mobile prop, smashed his way over for a try. We scored next with a fantastic Ieuan Evans try in the corner making it 10–8, but a Paul Williams try pegged us back again before a Paul Thorburn penalty extended their lead.

We eventually lost by a single point, 13–14, which was hard to take, but I suppose Neath deserved their win. They had had an outstanding season. I would go on to spend a lot of time with Neath's Huw Richards, Phil Pugh, Kevin Phillips, Mike Richards and the infamous Jeremy Pugh, who I had also played with in the front row for Brecknockshire County, whilst touring with Wales. They were good people.

CHAPTER 6

Getting Closer via the 'Friendly' Islands!

I LOOK BACK upon my rugby career as a journey which I approached without any expectations, as I have said previously. I just wanted to take advantage of any opportunities that came my way and see how far I could go.

Having established myself with Llanelli, the first real inclination that I could play international rugby came from a surprising direction – Scotland! With a name like Buchanan, which has its origins in Stirlingshire, I suppose it was understandable but I did not know of any kilt-wearing ancestors!

I had played against Glasgow and District at Stradey Park early in my Llanelli career, and was approached not long after the game by a representative of the Scottish Rugby Union enquiring about my eligibility for Scotland. I did start to look into it but thought to myself, if I was to play international rugby it would only be for Wales. So I said, 'Thanks, but no thanks.'

Technically, with my heritage, I could have played for England but that was never an option as far as I was concerned. I have always considered myself Welsh and would have turned England down, although I never felt any part of that hatred towards England that does exist in Wales, and I'm even a closet England football supporter.

I wasn't being arrogant in thinking that I was going to play for Wales, but there was a lot of talk about me 'arriving on the scene' and being a different type of prop to what was around at the time – more of a ball-handler, a runner and a tackler – and people were pushing for me to have an opportunity. That chance had yet to materialise, but I realised that at least I was in the frame if my name was being mentioned. I knew that I just needed to keep playing and plugging away at it.

My confidence was growing and the game against the touring Australians was a turning point. I had held my own in the scrums and things started going my way after that game. It gave me the belief that I could compete against international Test players and the Welsh selectors must have agreed with me because I was picked on the bench for the Wales B side against Spain a few months later.

Wales B (or Wales A as it was later renamed for whatever reason) is another facet of Welsh rugby that has fallen by the wayside of professionalism, but it used to be a valuable vehicle for giving players a chance to prove that they could bridge the gap between club and international rugby. England still have a second team, the Saxons, and it suits them when you look at the players that come through the system. Perhaps it's a financial decision with the WRU.

The match against Spain took place at the Brewery Field in Bridgend, and when I look back at the players who were in that team – Paul Moriarty, Ieuan Evans, Mark Davies (now on the medical team for the international side), Jonathan Griffiths and Mark Douglas – it gives you some idea of how useful it was.

The front row was Tim Jones (London Welsh), Steve Davies (South Wales Police) and Peter Francis (Maesteg). Obviously, I would have liked to have been in the starting line-up but Tim Jones was regarded as a very good loose-head. I first came across Tim at London Welsh when playing for Llanelli – I had been changed over to the tight-head for this game and from the kick-off to the final whistle I collapsed every scrum, being frightened of going up in the air or backwards. My tactics led to Tim asking if there was any chance of me and him playing. I replied, 'There's no way I am going up or back, so the answer is no!'

*

Games away to Maesteg on a cold, wet Wednesday night aren't usually memorable occasions but I will never forget playing up there in 1986. However, it has nothing to do with the game itself. An hour or so before kick-off I was out on the pitch and was approached by a journalist called Gareth Hughes, who congratulated me for being named in the Wales squad for the tour to the South Sea Islands. This was the first I had heard of the announcement. I felt as if I wanted to run back in and phone my wife and my parents but there was a game to be played and that had to wait for later. That moment, where I was and who told me, has always stuck with me.

Wales hadn't been on a major tour for 20 years or so, but the WRU knew that the World Cup in Australia and New Zealand was coming up the following year and it was all about preparing for that – there was a lot of excitement surrounding it all. While I was initially over the moon on hearing the news, quite a few things happened to me between the announcement of the squad and my getting on that aeroplane.

It all started not long after the announcement. I came home from work and didn't feel at all well. I told my wife and went straight to bed. She called the doctor and he told me I had bronchitis. I spent the next two weeks in bed, which wasn't like me at all – I had never been off work before.

When I started to recover I began playing rugby again but found that I was short of breath very quickly and struggled to get around the field. I went to see a specialist, who examined me and gave me different types of steroids. I told him I had been selected to tour the South Seas with Wales. He said, 'Forget it. You're breathing capacity is down to 40 per cent. There's no way you'll be able to play international rugby.' It was a real downer and I was panic stricken.

I got in my car and, as I was driving home, I thought of Keith Hughes. He was a doctor at the surgery in Ystradgynlais and had played for Llanelli and Wales in the 1970s – surely he would understand my situation.

I drove straight to the surgery, parked and ran inside and told the receptionist I had to see Dr Hughes immediately. I was ordered to sit and wait, and after 20 minutes he came out and said, 'What the hell is the matter?'

I followed him into his room and explained what had happened, how I had been for these tests and had been on a running machine and puffing air through a tube. I showed him the diagnosis that my illness was probably pneumonia which had left me with asthma.

I will never forget his response. He told me to put the medication I had been given on his desk and he picked them up one by one and said, 'Bin. Bin. Bin. You can't take that pump, take the blue one.'

I said, 'What am I supposed to do?'

He replied, 'David Hemery is asthmatic and he won an Olympic Gold Medal in the 400 metres. And there are several players in that Wales team who have asthma. It does not interfere with anything. You may find that cold air affects you with your running but you just need to focus on getting back into training and pushing yourself and taking your pump.'

I took his advice and went back to Llanelli. In the first four or five games I would go to the toilet to take my pump without anyone noticing. But there were obviously certain signs that things weren't quite right, and eventually Alan Lewis approached me and said, 'Look, I know you've been ill but you really need to start getting your fitness back up.'

It was more to do with my adjusting to the medication and actually learning how to use the pump itself. Once I had found the right levels for me, I didn't struggle for breath as much. If you get it right, it does improve your airways.

Then I started looking around the changing room and realised that there were quite a few players using these pumps – Jonathan Davies is a classic example, he was asthmatic. Then the boys who weren't asthmatic started asking me if they could have a puff! I told them it's something I have got to take for my chest and not something to be taken lightly.

I faced a huge dilemma – did I tell the Welsh Rugby Union? In the end I didn't. You think that you are going to be OK. I wasn't silly enough to make myself available if I knew for sure that I wasn't fit enough. Dr Hughes had reassured me and it was just a case of learning how to deal with my new condition.

It was quite a roller-coaster ride until I finally got out there and, fortunately, because it was such a warm climate my asthma didn't bother me.

In time I tended to grow out of it, which does happen, and although my lung capacity has never returned to 100 per cent, it improved quite considerably. I don't think I ever reached the levels of fitness I had enjoyed before becoming ill.

*

I didn't really know anything about the type of rugby and what was ahead of me, but whoever described Fiji, Tonga and Samoa as the Friendly Islands had never stepped onto a rugby field to play against them! While I can't fault the people – they are lovely and so hospitable – when they cross that whitewash they become crazed warriors who think the opposition has come to invade their land and tear down their villages!

It soon became apparent that those who thought that it would be a flamboyant, touch-rugby style of play – my wife thought I would be packing sun cream and bathers, spending my time beneath palm trees on golden sand – were to be rudely awoken. I can honestly say that it proved to be the most violent rugby environment I have ever played in. The rugby was physical and challenging, and you were aware that all the time you were being assessed as to how you dealt with that type of environment ahead of the Rugby World Cup.

The tour started in Fiji and I was selected to play in the second game, against an Eastern Select XV, at the national stadium in Suva.

The first thing that hit you – and we were hit by lots of things on that tour, mainly boots, elbows and fists – was the heat. We wore the old heavy, woollen jerseys to play in temperatures north of 90 degrees – you were looking for a scissors to cut the sleeves off to try and get air. You were perspiring so much you probably lost half a stone of weight in sweat before you got out of the changing room door. Even the home team were looking for shade.

They kicked off. I jumped to receive the ball, and their hooker dived like a torpedo from three metres away to hit the back of my legs, sending me spinning in the air. By the time I landed most of the Fijian pack had arrived to trample all over me.

They didn't care where they put their boots and there is no doubt that they were there to hurt you and, quite literally, leave their mark. I can remember having to move my head to narrowly miss boots coming down either side of me.

It wasn't a good game to be part of as we lost 29–13 – our only defeat of the tour. I wasn't particularly happy with my performance. I felt that I could have done better, but the truth was I had been badly shaken by the kicking I got at that first kick-off – the shirt had quite literally been ripped off my back – and I didn't really recover in that game.

I had to go for stitches afterwards and got chatting to the doctor. I said, 'You play your rugby a bit rough here.'

He replied, 'If you think this is rough, just wait until you get to Tonga!' And he was right!

*

As with all tours, there were also light-hearted moments. On one occasion we were at a function and there was a Welsh-speaking expat who had come along because he had heard that the Welsh team was on tour and wanted to have a conversation in Welsh. The boys called me over. As I was from the upper Swansea Valley they thought I was fluent, but my Welsh is basic to say the least. We started chatting and he said, 'I'm originally from Ystradgynlais.' My immediate thought was that I had been set up but it turned out that his father used to be the station master in Ystradgynlais and he had moved to Fiji 25 years previously, settled there and now owned a small island called Orchid Island.

He still had relatives living in Ystrad and Abercrave, the Watkins family. He was a nice person who took me and a couple of the boys out fishing – we all have a photograph, sat holding up the same tuna fish pretending we had caught it! That's the kind of friendships and memories you forge on rugby tours and they last a lifetime.

*

I hadn't been involved in the Test against Fiji, which we won 15–22. David Pickering had a nasty head injury following one ruck – he was very lucky that there was a neurosurgeon actually at the game and received excellent care straightaway. However, as I mentioned earlier, I don't think that he ever really recovered from that injury.

I was handed a start in the next match, against the Tonga President's XV. Just before kick-off I was standing behind Richard Moriarty, waiting to shake hands with the King of

Tonga, and looked across to this six-foot two-inch player, with a shaved head and a big, bushy moustache, staring back at me with wild eyes.

I said to Dickie, 'Look at that guy.'

'You're marking him,' he replied. 'He's their tight-head.' His name was Latu Va'eno, and I still have nightmares about him today!

After just 20 minutes, three of our boys had to leave the field and this guy was the culprit each time. We held a team talk and it was agreed that we had to do something about him.

'Has anyone got an elephant gun?' I asked. It was the only way we were going to stop him! A plan was hatched and all I can say is that he was severely dealt with in the next ruck.

To his immense credit, he got up with blood pouring from a large gash on the side of his head. They tried to stop the blood but the more they put the magic sponge on it, the more the blood flowed out. It was horrendous.

I have never stamped on anyone in my life – I just wouldn't do it – but for some unknown reason he thought that it was me.

He looked directly at me, pointed, and said, 'You're dead man.'

I thought, 'Now I'm in trouble.'

Fortunately, his medical team forced him to leave the field. I have never been so glad to see someone go off in my life. We managed to go on and win the game, 9–13, but afterwards our coaches, Tony Gray and Derek Quinnell, told the Tongan management that the level of violence that had been directed towards us was unacceptable.

They obviously paid no attention to the warning as the Test match against Tonga, which came next, was one of the most violent games Wales has ever faced – it was pure GBH. I hadn't been picked but it was almost a case of, for once, being glad that I wasn't out there on the field of play!

Although there were incidents throughout, there was one

almighty punch up, initiated by Tonga, which saw Welsh jerseys laid out all over the field! Bleddyn Bowen was chased and ran into the crowd – and was thrown back onto the pitch! I believe three of our players had to go to hospital during the game – at one stage an ambulance drove onto the field!

In all seriousness, the levels of violence far exceeded anything that was acceptable. It was well documented at the end of the tour that we had been the victims of foul play to put it mildly. I know Tony Gray was furious once more.

The game wasn't shown live on television because of the distance and limits of technology back then. But S4C did have a film crew out there. However, the video tapes disappeared – conspiracy theorists can make of that what they wish, but if I was a Tongan I wouldn't have wanted people analysing what went on.

Maybe we upset them before the game. As we were introduced to the King of Tonga, a rather large gentleman, someone stated the fact in Welsh, causing a few of the players to laugh out loud.

*

There was only one game when we moved on to Samoa, the Test match, which we won fairly convincingly 4–32, but once again I wasn't involved. You need to remember that you were only allowed two replacements on the bench back then and they would go with one forward and one back.

I wasn't too disappointed as I had pulled on the red jersey of Wales and was getting closer. The Cardiff loose-head, Jeff Whitefoot, a resilient player who rarely got injured, was ahead of me in the pecking order, and I had a lot of respect for Jeff. He was a good scrummager, although I felt I was probably a better all-round rugby player than him.

My scrummaging had definitely improved and, each season, I felt that I was getting stronger and more experienced. I still sometimes found certain props, of different sizes with different techniques challenging – it doesn't matter what people tell you about the front row being the place where the dull chaps end up; it's more of a thinking game than you realise. It's about technique and strength but you also have to think your way around it.

Also, I guess people's opinion of me was that I wasn't quite the hard-nosed scrummager that was required for international rugby, and I had to gain that experience to make sure that when my opportunity came I could take it. I just needed that break. The tour had given me a taste of what to expect and I was determined to step up to the next level.

That came the following season, 1987, when I made it into the match day squad and found myself on the bench for the Five Nations (as it was back then, as Italy had yet to be invited to the top table).

CHAPTER 7

Playing for Wales in the Rugby World Cup

ALTHOUGH I DIDN'T get capped on the South Seas tour, I knew that I was firmly in the frame and approached the following season, 1986/87, with real hope of making that final breakthrough. I just had to convince the selectors to pick me!

The Wales coach wasn't responsible for selecting the side, as is the system today. The responsibility fell to a panel of five selectors known to all as the Big Five. They obviously had their own opinions on the type of player they were looking for and they would tour the grounds to run the rule over players. There was always someone there watching you play, and someone would give you the nod that they were in the stand. You knew that it was all about your performance and you had to perform every time you played.

The selection of the Wales team, especially as Wales played far fewer games back then and you could say they were more eagerly anticipated, was something of a national pastime and often the favourite topic of debate in workplaces, pubs and rugby clubs across the country. Everyone was an expert! You would hear mutterings on where you stood in the pecking order and it was usually played out in the press – sometimes a rugby journalist would favour you and you would read things like, 'The Big Five can't ignore Buchanan any more.' What pleased me most was my peers were beginning to ask why I was being overlooked, with the Wales tight-head Stuart Evans asking one journalist, 'How isn't Buchanan in the team?'

I realised that there was a growing call for me to be given a chance. I think it was all down to us playing a brand of rugby in Llanelli that was ball in, ball out, and we were away. Moving all the time. It was more in line with how rugby is played today.

Generally, props were predominantly there to scrummage and lift in the lineout, but we played a different all-action style of rugby. As I have said, rugby, when I played, was very much a set-piece orientated game. If you could dominate the scrum and lineout, you tended to win the game. It was hard yards, intimidation and fierce rucking. You never saw 15, 20 phases of possession like you see today. I would've loved to have played in the modern game. I think it would've suited me down to the ground.

*

My ambitions were fuelled by the news that I had been selected to play in the Wales trials just before the start of the international season. Things looked to be finally going my way when I was selected in the Probables. You had the Probables (as the name suggests the most likely to be picked) in red, playing against the less likely Possibles in white. Both teams were very close and all players, who were mainly of equal ability, had a lot to prove. The red team played to hang on to the jersey while the white team played to get the jersey! If I was honest, I would rather have been in the Possibles as they were probably hungrier for it and would throw everything they had at the Probables who were there to be knocked off their perch.

The trial games were seldom classics and never pretty. As you can imagine, there were always quite a few players with a point to prove and you always knew that all hell would break loose! I remember one trial – I played in three in all – Dai Waters, the Newport second row, was laid out in the first lineout. You had some big hitters going in.

Unfortunately, the trial didn't go well for me, and when they announced the side for the first game of the Five Nations, against France, Jeff Whitefoot was in ahead of me once more and I was named on the bench. I was obviously disappointed, but I never dwelt on the disappointments – once it was done it was done, and I moved on. I never forgot that I had never expected anything to begin with, having switched to rugby so late. I have also always believed that selection is just someone else's opinion and being left out did not mean that I wasn't good enough.

I wasn't alone in being disappointed travelling back to the upper Swansea Valley that day, as Huw Richards, the Neath second row from Abercrave, had also missed out on selection. There were a couple of occasions when we travelled back from trials together and called in at the White Horse in Glynneath for a consolatory beer and discussed how disappointed we were with our performances.

Despite being from Abercrave, Ystrad's fierce rivals, we often roomed together and got on very well. He will kill me for saying this; he often ironed my shirts for me as I was hopeless at it!

Huw had been capped on the South Seas tour against Tonga – he played four times for Wales but never completed 80 minutes. He came on twice as a replacement and was knocked out, carried off and sent off – there must be a quiz question there somewhere.

He was a good guy and good company and I call him a friend to this day.

*

I sat on the bench throughout the 1987 Five Nations Championship which was a deeply frustrating time. Unlike today, where if you are on the bench you are more or less guaranteed a cap as the coaches almost always send everyone on, replacements were only used if someone was genuinely injured, and usually a doctor would make sure! Also, players were reluctant to show they were injured, no one came off – they were frightened that if someone came on instead and played well, they wouldn't get back in the team. No one gave anyone a cap. Throughout the years before this time, and for a while after, players were very cautious about allowing another to have an opportunity in the Welsh jersey.

My first game was in Paris which was something of a dilemma as Alana was expecting our first child and was due that very week. Amy would kill me for saying this but I did say that if the baby did not arrive that week I was still on the plane! To my delight I was there for the birth as she arrived on the Tuesday.

During the game Serge Blanco put up a huge up-and-under, and when Paul Thorburn went to meet it half the French pack hit him. He dislocated his shoulder and off he went. I was sat next to Malcolm Dacey and said, 'I'll go on as fullback!' I had played my first-ever game of rugby in that position for Ystradgynlais seconds, remember!

It wasn't the start we would have wanted, and France won quite comfortably, 16–9.

The next game was at home against England. The atmosphere and whole occasion was amazing. I had played on the Arms Park in Cup finals but the ground was never quite full and was split between the two teams, so you didn't have the dominant singing of the hymns and arias or such a wall of noise. It was probably the most frustrating time I spent on the bench – I would've walked over broken glass to get on that field.

The game itself is quite infamous as there was one almighty

punch-up. Wade Dooley walloped Phil Davies in a lineout and broke his cheekbone, resulting in a huge brawl. They were a tough bunch.

England were overwhelming favourites going into the game, but Stuart Evans' famous try, and Mark Wyatt's five penalties, helped Wales secure a 19–12 victory.

A chance did come my way when it came to the away trip to Scotland, but I turned it down – with good reason. Stuart Evans, our tight-head, had damaged his ankle on the Thursday in training and the chairman of the Big Five, Rod Morgan, called me in and said, 'Look, Stuart has gone down, and we're going to have to bring another prop in. We would rather bring an out-and-out tight-head in but, before we do, how do you feel about it? Do you want to go over to the tight-head?'

I didn't quite know what to say but then he added, 'Remember, the World Cup is coming up. You're in the frame, you don't want to mess it up now.'

I said, 'Fine.'

So they flew up the Maesteg prop, Peter Francis. The poor guy must have felt that he never got off that aeroplane because he spent every scrum in the air!

We roomed together and he was devastated after the game. You couldn't wish to meet a nicer guy, I really did feel for him. It wasn't fair on him because he didn't have any time to settle into the set-up. He was up against a top British Lion in David Sole, and Scotland were a real handful.

I have to be honest, I reflected on that game and thought, 'That could've been me!'

Scotland won 21–15.

What was really unfair was that his wife and parents had driven up on the Friday night, so he was worried about them and had lots on his mind and didn't sleep well before the game.

At least he won a cap. He had done his hard yards with

Maesteg and was a well-respected prop on the circuit. It just didn't work out for him.

I had hoped to get a chance in the final game, against Ireland in Cardiff, but it was not to be both for myself and Wales, as we lost 11–15.

Although I took no comfort from the fact, Wales had only won once during the championship and came second from bottom – but still above England!

*

Although I was gutted not to win that elusive first cap during the Five Nations Championship, my disappointment was soon forgotten when I was named in the Wales squad to play in the first-ever Rugby World Cup at the end of May that year. I was the only uncapped player in the original squad and was one of just two loose-heads named – the other was Jeff Whitefoot – so I knew that I would never have a better opportunity to play for my country.

There was a huge amount of publicity around the first Rugby World Cup, and the fact that it was being held in Australia and New Zealand was exciting to us northern hemisphere boys. At that stage no one knew that it would grow into what it is today – I believe it's the third largest global sporting event behind the football World Cup and the Olympics – but we knew that it was the start of something special.

Once the squad had been named, we were taken away for a couple of training weekends in Tenby, staying at the St Brides Hotel in Saundersfoot, something that had never happened before. It was cutting edge!

We would play and train all day Saturday and all day Sunday. (Club rugby training at the time consisted of two one-and-a-half-hour sessions on a Tuesday and Thursday, or Monday if there was a game on the Wednesday.) On the Monday you couldn't move, you were as stiff as a board. We just weren't physically prepared to be in that kind of environment; it was something new, it was something different.

We would be running on the beach in the mornings and training all day, but we still had a few pints in the evenings and our girlfriends and wives would come down and join us on the Saturday night. It was more about team building than anything else, and we all became quite friendly as a group. They were a great bunch and there was no animosity in the squad. To be fair, we became more like a club side than an international team in terms of how well we bonded together. We all got on well and had a lot of fun together off the field.

During another training camp Lynn Davies, Lynn the Leap, the Olympic Gold Medallist, would try to get us forwards to sprint properly on the track – we were running on our heels rather than on our toes. We were like a load of ducks running but at least I was a lot quicker than all the other props!

It was interesting to have my old teammate, Derek Quinnell, as our forwards coach. He never let me off the hook mind you, and was always on to me. He was so well respected and his knowledge of the game – as a Lions winner over New Zealand – was well known, but he also deserves credit for his coaching ability, he was advanced in his thinking at that time. Tony Gray also deserves a huge amount of credit. He remains the most successful Welsh coach when it comes to World Cups – and I think he was treated rather poorly.

There were five Swansea Valley boys in the squad – me, Huw Richards; Bleddyn Bowen and Robert Jones (two recognised international names and great guys from Trebanos, a few miles down the valley) and Kevin Hopkins, not to mention the team manager being a certain Clive Rowlands from Upper Cwmtwrch! It was quite an accomplishment for such a small area and makes a great question in a rugby quiz, but not as good as one relating back to the day Ystradgynlais met Swansea in the Cup.

Our World Cup captain was Richard Moriarty, the player I had stood opposite during lineouts in the Schweppes Cup at the Recreation Ground in Ystradgynlais six years previously. And if that wasn't a remarkable thing in itself, one of our centres that day, Kevin Hopkins, had also made the leap from west Wales to the World Cup, via Swansea; quite a feather in the cap for Ystradgynlais Rugby Club.

Also in the Swansea squad that day were fellow World Cup players Malcolm Dacey and Gareth Roberts.

I was glad that Clive Rowlands was our team manager. To me, he is an exceptional rugby man. He's done it all, and if he tells you something you listen. He was very approachable and knew the game inside out and was highly respected around the world. He's done everything from captaining Wales to coaching them and managing the British and Irish Lions. We all had a huge regard for Clive and his opinions.

He had seen me elevate myself through the ranks. Remember, he had come along to deliver a team talk before Ystradgynlais played against Swansea and Llanelli in the Schweppes Cup. What's more, he had his Top Cat sports shop in Ystalyfera and I always bought my boots from him – until I was given them for free!

To be honest with you, I took any freebies I could as the time off from work was always unpaid and we never had much from the WRU – I think it was a £15 daily allowance. You knew that you were going to lose money but I, like most people, would have paid to play for my country – I would have swum to New Zealand.

*

Wales were drawn in the same pool as Ireland, Canada and our 'good friends' Tonga. I knew that if I stayed clear of any type of injury the chances were that I would almost certainly be capped.

We began with a 13–6 win over Ireland, but the selectors had kept faith with Whitefoot.

The next game was against Tonga, and as we were on the bus heading to our next base, Palmerston North, Clive Rowlands read the team out and he said my name first. I had finally been picked! It was quite a moment, and as I was the only uncapped player in the original squad everyone made a fuss of congratulating me.

When the news filtered back home I was inundated with telegrams – that's how long ago it was! There was one from my parents, from Llanelli and Ystradgynlais, and lots of the west Wales clubs, including our fierce rivals Abercrave! As well as from the boys at the colliery. The television commentators Huw Llywelyn Davies and Lyn Davies even bought me a bottle of champagne.

After the initial excitement settled down I began focusing on the game, and when I looked at the Tongan line-up I was immensely relieved to discover that my old foe, Latu Va'eno, wasn't there.

I will never forget running out – feeling a bit gutted that it was in our changed strip of green as Tonga had won the toss to wear red – and singing 'Hen Wlad Fy Nhadau' at the top of my voice. The emotion was incredible – I just wish my family had been there in person to see it.

We started really well, and were giving Tonga a really hard time in the scrums when the prop I was playing against started limping around. Soon after, this huge roar went up in the crowd – I knew it was him.

We were about to go down for a scrum, but the referee stopped the game and the prop I was marking went off and on came Va'eno.

As he was running on, no word of a lie, the referee, Kerry Fitzgerald (Australia), who sadly passed away in December 1991, turned to me and said, 'Watch yourself mate, this one is absolutely crazy.'

He ran on the field looking like Popeye. He worked as a cane cutter in the sugar fields and his arms were pumped up like cannonballs, and his eyes were popping out of his head. He stepped into their front row and I thought to myself, 'This is my chance!' As we were going down to engage, I head-butted him!

The scrum broke up in a big brawl, with me staying as close to him as possible, throwing punches left, right and centre. The referee finally restored order and pulled us both to one side and gave us the finest lecture before warning Va'eno that if he so much as looked at anyone again, he would be straight off. It was a huge piece of kidology on my part; the referee knew his reputation and I had conned the ref into thinking he had started it. The ref sent him away and called me close and said, 'I will keep an eye on him the best I can, but watch yourself because he will be out to get you. Don't retaliate whatever you do, leave him to me.'

Thankfully, the rest of the game settled down without further incident and we won 29–16, although the scoreline didn't reflect what a battle it had been.

If you have any doubts about that, just ask our flying wing Glenn Webbe. He scored a hat-trick but doesn't remember a thing after his first two tries because he almost had his head knocked off by a flying no-arms tackle that left him out cold. Incredibly, by today's safety standards, he carried on because of the only two replacements rule, and scored a brilliant, length of the field solo try. When he finally came round properly, some time after the game, the management told him they were sending him home because he was concussed!

That evening Steve 'Wally' Blackmore, Stuart Evans and myself went out to celebrate my first cap. We entered this bar, which was upstairs, to be greeted by the amazing sight of a crowd of people cowering in one corner while the Tongan prop, Va'eno, took up the rest of the room kicking tables and chairs around.

I turned to Stuart, who was still negotiating the stairs as he was on crutches after breaking his ankle in the game, and said, 'Let's go somewhere else, that prop is here!'

'There's three of us,' he replied.

I said, 'It will take the three of us! He's up there and he's had a good drink, I'm telling you now.'

'Don't worry, we'll sort it out.'

'OK,' I said, 'but I can run away. You can't!' We walked into the room and he spotted us.

'Here we go,' I thought.

The next thing, he walks over with his fingers in four pints, bangs them on the table and says, 'You drink with me.'

'Of course,' we all said, and sat down.

Then he looked at me, leaned his head forwards, pointing to this huge scar on his head and said, 'Tonga. That was you.'

For one moment I almost said, 'No, no, it wasn't me! It was ...'

What I actually said was, 'No. It wasn't me. I don't stamp on people.'

I heard a few years down the line that he was jailed after biting another prop's ear off!

He was a little bit of a crazy horse.

*

Although I was happy with my performance, Jeff Whitefoot was brought back in for the final group game against Canada, which we won 40–9, setting up a quarter-final showdown with England!

I have always said that if you are going to have some luck, you need to be in the right place at the right time, and I couldn't have timed what happened next any better. I was probably always going to play against Tonga but Jeff was the number one loose-head and would in all likelihood have played against England, but he was forced to return home due to a family emergency. Although I felt terrible for Jeff, that opened the way for me to play in the quarter-final of the Rugby World Cup... against our greatest rivals!

I had never been so motivated for a game in my life – it was, after all, by far the biggest game of my career, as it was for all the boys. I listened to my Walkman on the way to the ground – I'm afraid to say that it was the 'Eye of the Tiger' song from *Rocky* – to wind myself up. I think the animosity against the English is just a characteristic of being Welsh – if you grew up in Wales and played international rugby, you wanted to play against England, and our supporters like nothing better than to beat them!

England were the favourites going into the game, especially as we had a cobbled-together front row, and I don't think many people gave us a chance. I was only winning my second cap. David Young, who happened to be playing club rugby in Australia, was called up to make his Test debut as a raw 19 year old, along with Richard Webster, the flanker. What those two youngsters achieved was terrific, and you could tell that they were earmarked for great things in their future careers and they both went on to become British Lions.

At hooker was Alan Phillips, who had been flown out as a replacement, so he was a third-choice hooker. Credit where credit's due, Thumper, as Alan Phillips is known, was a British Lion, and with all his experience he looked after us and offered words of encouragement throughout the game – he really drove us on.

We were determined to get into the English from the start. There was a lineout early on and they tapped the ball back and I went through and fell on the ball – and received the biggest kicking. I had placed myself in a stupid position and was lucky not to be seriously hurt. One of the English forwards said to me afterwards, 'How the hell did you get up from that?' It dawned on me that this was going to be a really tough environment.

Take it from me, it's never going to be easy when you play

against England – they were a lot more physical and robust. I wouldn't call them dirty players, but they were physical and a bloody good outfit. Players like Mike Teague, Dean Richards and Peter Winterbottom in there, an all British Lions back row, all great players. Tough guys.

I was up against Gary Pearce and had faced him before when Llanelli played Northampton, so I wasn't intimidated by him. Then you had the 'Pitbull' Brian Moore at hooker, and Paul Rendell, the 'Judge', on the loose-head. As it turned out, the scrum went well, and one led to a try for us.

One incident stands out for me because I was in the middle of an alleged dangerous tackle which, had it taken place today, would have given viewers time to boil the kettle and make a sandwich by the time the TMOs reviewed the footage! Mike Harrison, their captain, had come through from the wing on a dummy scissors and I was there and just absolutely poleaxed him. The referee penalised me, but it wasn't a dirty tackle. I don't understand why he penalised me; it was one of those tackles that looked far worse than it actually was. I didn't go high – the video of it is actually on the internet somewhere, so you can judge for yourself.

As it turned out, the result sounded fairly comprehensive, with tries by Gareth Roberts, John Devereux and Robert Jones helping us win 16–3. Some later labelled it the worst game of the tournament, but not if you were a Welsh supporter and certainly not if you were a member of the team which beat England to make it to a World Cup semi-final!

My initial reaction at the final whistle was one of relief, and then my thoughts turned to my family and friends back home. That was the only downside; we didn't have the travelling support in huge numbers as you see today but I could picture the boys back in the rugby club punching the air with delight and getting the next round in even though it was early morning! When we finally arrived home, I remember someone complaining to me they had to get up at stupid o'clock in the morning to watch because of the time difference.

It was exciting for my family and all my friends watching me playing – it is such a big honour to pull the red shirt on and to beat England, and even though it wasn't a great game it's something that will live with me for ever. It may have lacked quality, but it didn't matter, we were through to the semi-final and I felt a terrific sense of achievement.

*

When I discovered that we were set to face New Zealand in the semi-final, I was genuinely excited and looked forward to it. Clive Rowlands was at his inspiring best and was telling us that the All Blacks were only skin and bone like the rest of us.

It may appear strange to some, but following the game we went down to the famous Australian Gold Coast for a bit of rest and recuperation before facing New Zealand. I doubt it would ever happen in this day and age. We still had training sessions down there, but it was a different environment. Yes, we had a blowout but it was only one night on the beer.

Staying in the same hotel as us was the England midfielder, Bryan Robson, who joined us for a drink. All I will say is, whatever you think about football players, he more than held his own!

It was a great couple of days and we really enjoyed ourselves. Kevin Phillips, Huw Richards and I were in the bar at the end of the night with Clive Rowlands – we could easily have been at The George in Cwmtwrch! When Clive, who had been telling us that he had decided to lose weight and was on a diet, announced that he was calling it a night, we formulated a plan.

The next morning we ordered breakfast to be sent to his room with everything we could think of! We hid in the corridor, and when the waiter delivered it to his room on a trolley, we heard him say, 'I haven't ordered breakfast. It must be a mistake.' He then stuck his head out of the door, looked up and down the corridor and, not seeing us hiding, said, 'Well, seeing as you're here, you might as well bring it in.'

Somehow, he found out it was us and reminds me to this day that we were responsible for him giving up his diet!

Even in hindsight, I do not believe that our little trip to the Gold Coast was a bad idea. The whole World Cup experience was something brand-new and the pressure on us was quite immense – we had never faced anything like it before from a rugby point of view and we needed a release. After all, everything was in place. We had done the training by then and we had come together as a team. We needed to break the monotony of the tour, of the routine, get away and relax and recharge our batteries. It was the case of, 'Boys, have a blowout. Let off some steam and come back tomorrow ready to focus on the job which lies ahead. Get your head on.'

*

The semi-final took place in Ballymore, Brisbane, which meant we had the crowd on our side – all the Aussies were shouting for Wales. Unfortunately, that didn't affect the All Blacks one bit; they were a professional bunch and ready for this World Cup.

I genuinely went into the game believing that we had the chance to win and, more importantly, we wanted to win. But, we knew that we had to be at our best and things had to go our way. Without a shadow of a doubt, New Zealand were an immensely talented rugby team. We were under pressure from the start. It was relentless rucks, mauls and scrums – they were powerhouses. I remember tackling their prop, Steve McDowall, and I'm sure every member of the pack, and some of the backs, ran right over the top of me. It wasn't the same level of dirtiness as we had experienced against Tonga, but they played harder.

New Zealand scored eight tries to win 49–6. Our only reply was a solitary try by John Devereux, converted by Paul Thorburn. The game's biggest talking point, apart from the score, was the punch-up. There was a lineout and Huw Richards gave Gary Whetton a wallop and a fight broke out. I came around and saw 'Buck' Shelford hitting Huw from the side which knocked him flat out. I threw a left hook at Shelford. It was instinctive, I just jumped in. Huw was a friend and I just reacted. I wasn't in there long because somebody hit me from the side, and I went out of the side door. I got back up on my feet very quickly and went back in but by then everybody was trying to cool it down. The outcome of the mêlée was that Huw Richards was sent off.

My actions led to the only compliment I've ever had from Neath's Brian Thomas. He told me after the World Cup, 'Fair play, at least you had a go. It wasn't much of go but at least you tried.'

I replied, 'Brian, coming from you, that's a compliment.'

Huw was totally devastated after the game. But, truth be told, we were in trouble long before the sending-off and it didn't really affect the result. I think he was hard done by, I really do. Shelford should have been sent off as well. If one was sent off, then both should have gone. They were a superb rugby team, and they were determined. If I were a betting man, I would've put my house on them winning that World Cup – which they did of course.

*

In the aftermath of the game Clive Rowlands famously declared, 'We will have to go back to beating England every year.' That ruffled an awful lot of feathers but that was Clive's mischievous side for you – you couldn't meet a more passionate Welshman.

We were obviously very disappointed with the result, but we had no time to feel sorry for ourselves because our World Cup wasn't quite over. We had one more job to do with a third/fourth place play-off against the losers of the other semi-final, between Australia and France, less than five days away.

We also realised a number of the side wouldn't play again because they were going to change the team and involve those who had been on the periphery. I wasn't sure whether they were going to pick me because, with only two fit props left in the squad, they had flown the Newport prop John Rawlins in. But, he pulled a hamstring in the first training session – once again one man's misfortune was another man's luck. John never did win a cap after that. As it turned out, I believe only myself and Richard Moriarty survived in the pack.

Personally, I was really up for the game – I wanted to play. It was the same for the whole squad; we were extremely disappointed with the scoreline against New Zealand. We genuinely believed we were a better team than that result showed, and we had a chance to take something home with us if we could only beat Australia.

In fairness, I suppose we were far more up for the game than Australia. As co-hosts they had been expected to win the World Cup, so their disappointment must have been greater. Another factor in our favour was the play-off took place in New Zealand, in Rotorua, and this time we had the entire New Zealand crowd on our side.

The Aussie pack tried to soften us up early on by getting stuck into us, but that probably backfired as they had a player sent off quite early on in the game. When you lose a player it can either galvanise a team or demoralise you. Fortunately, I believe the sending off weakened Australia. Remember, I had faced Australia with Llanelli and had won, but to beat them a second time in a World Cup third-place play-off would be even more special. The whole game hinged on the final kick as Paul Thorburn attempted to convert a last-minute corner flag try by Adrian Hadley right on the touchline.

The score at that point was 21–22 to Australia. We all knew that if it went over we had won, because it was the last action of the game. Knowing what a great goal kicker Paul was, I knew that there was a good chance he would do it. He was so prolific and accurate. In all honesty, I can say I was confident he would do it but, all the same, I could not bring myself to watch! I just turned my back and prayed for the best. To say I was delighted when I heard the crowd roar as it sailed between the posts is an understatement. It in no way took away the disappointment of the semi-final – it was our performance more than the result which left us disappointed – but it certainly went a long way to regaining our self-respect. It was tremendous to have been able to make amends so soon after what had been a massive low point.

There was obviously relief that the tournament was over. We could hold our heads up high and we could relax and have a few beers. One of the highlights came on the flight home. At an overnight stop we met Tom Jones in the airport bar. He was genuinely pleased to meet us, and all the boys posed for pictures alongside him. In turns we bought rounds of drinks, with one for Tom every time. When Steve Sutton asked Tom what the value of the ring he wore on his little finger was, he replied, 'Not sure, but very expensive.' This prompted Steve to say, 'It's your turn to buy the next round then.' To which Tom replied that he didn't have any money on him, and he was waiting for his son to pick him up from the airport. We then got round to asking, 'What are the chances of going round to your house for a drink tonight?' Tom quickly disappeared!

Our celebratory mood was certainly reflected by the nation back home. Kevin Hopkins and I were treated like returning heroes, and there was a big party at Ystradgynlais Rugby Club, and at all the boys' local clubs across Wales.

As elated as I felt, I was soon brought back down to earth when I returned to work. My first job underground was to fix a gasket on the pump in the main sump. It was a difficult job as I had to do the repair in situ, as the machinery weighed several tons and couldn't be moved easily. I was up to my waist in water and it was a race against time because the water was still coming into the sump. The manager came down and looked at me in the water and said, 'There you are Buchanan. If you had won the World Cup you would have had a job on the surface.'

CHAPTER 8

Back Down to Earth
and a Surprise Call-up

AFTER HELPING WALES to third place in the Rugby World Cup, I quite justifiably believed my international career was finally taking off. I found myself named in the Probables for the Wales trials once more the following season but, when they named the team for the first game, away to England, I wasn't even included on the bench. I was in good company however, because they also dropped Paul Thorburn. It seemed particularly harsh as Paul had won the game against Australia with his brilliant touchline conversion, yet he found himself dumped out of the team. The selectors brought in a young Tony Clement at fullback, going for more pace and an attacking threat I suppose.

Jeff Whitefoot had dropped right out of the picture and I had expected to become number one. But Staff Jones, the Pontypool loose-head, had recovered from a long-term injury and was chosen ahead of me. To be fair to Staff, he was a British Lion and well regarded as a top scrummager. They still regarded the scrum as a major cornerstone of the team. However, no disrespect to Staff, he was never a ball handler, he was old school.

I was obviously disappointed, even more so as the Lions tour to Australia was on the horizon and I knew this would damage any hopes I had of making the squad. I had already suffered

Sibling school days – me with my brother, Robert, and sister, Beverley
© TJ Davies

First love – my horse Chief

CWM WANDERERS A.F.C. 1973-74 (Grand Slam)
LEAGUE CHAMPIONS, PREMIER CUP WINNERS, OPEN CUP WINNERS & CHAMPION CUP WINNERS
Standing:- Ref, Wayne Davies, Roy Brittain, Lynne Walters, Dilwyn Davies, Gerwyn Howells, Anthony Buchanan, Robert Buchanan, Brian 'Joko' Jones, Jeffrey Stevens, David 'Coslett' Davies.
Kneeling:- Adrian Jones, Brian Morris, Brian 'Dal' Jones, Cecil John Smith, Neil Morgan.
(Chairman) (Captain) (Vice Captain) (Secretary)

In goal – the mighty Cwm Wanderers (I'm in the green jersey next to Tarzan in yellow)

Wedding bells – me and my beautiful bride Alana, with my parents Margaret and Jack (left) and in-laws Euros and Harriett (right)

© TJ Davies

Most promising player – despite taking to rugby relatively late, I soon showed potential

© TJ Davies

Lineout king – me jumping in a lineout for Ystradgynlais in our Cup game against Swansea

Ystrad Firsts – the Ystradgynlais side which narrowly lost to Swansea in the Cup, and I'm second from the right in the back row

© TJ Davies

Cup magic – marking Derek Quinnell at the back of the lineout in our Cup game against my future first-class club

Ystrad girls – our brilliant ladies' section offering support from the stand (Alana is sat seventh from the right)

© TJ Davies

Collier boy – taking centre stage with my Treforgan Colliery colleagues
© Geraint Burgess

Playing Pooler – it looks like I was just about to swing a right hook, but I always enjoyed playing against Pontypool

Facing the Whites – a derby against Swansea was always guaranteed to be a feisty affair with a sell-out crowd

On trial – Welsh trials were always keenly fought, but Mike Griffiths goes a bit too far in this one

© Huw Evans Agency

Wearing the red of Wales – running out behind Richard Moriarty for my first appearance in a Welsh jersey against the Fiji President's XV

Bags packed – getting ready for the 1987 Rugby World Cup with my wife Alana and new daughter Amy

© South Wales Evening Post

Me, Clive Rowlands and Kevin Phillips in New Zealand

Showing off the tuna fish caught while on our tour to Fiji

Me, Laurance, Phil Davies and Gareth Jenkins embark on our boating adventure in California

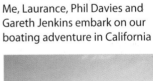

Being towed back after almost sinking

Laurance keen to take over the helm from me, while Phil enjoys a beer

Wales Rugby World Cup 1987 squad
© Huw Evans Agency

First cap – in the changing room with Ieuan Evans prior to making my full debut for my country at the Rugby World Cup against Tonga

Jubilant front row – Dai Young (left), Alan 'Thumper' Phillips and yours truly after beating England in the RWC quarter-final

Ystrad boys lift the cup – Kevin Hopkins and I eye up the RWC ahead of our semi-final against New Zealand

Nieces and nephews – (L–R) Heidi, Gareth, Rhian, Darrell, Jeremy and Craig, with baby Amy modelling my jerseys from the RWC

Returning hero – modelling my RWC caps with Alana and Amy

Ironing man – pictured with my friend and roommate, Huw Richards, who helped me iron my shirts, alongside Kevin Phillips, on the ill-fated 1988 New Zealand tour

Line of duty – injured quartet (L–R) Phil May, yours truly, Jeremy Pugh and Ieuan Evans on the brutal New Zealand tour

Becoming a Barbarian – lining up for the famous invitational side
© Huw Evans Agency

Team manger – Llanelli team photograph prior to the Welsh Cup final which was held in Bristol when the National Stadium was being rebuilt

Lifting the Cup – the last time I was involved in winning the Welsh Cup with Llanelli, 2010
© Riley Sports Photography

Family support – my daughter Adele meeting Scarlets and Wales outside-half, Stephen Jones

Cup kings – pictured before and after with my Ystradgynlais team and fellow coaches down at Stradey Park for the West Wales Plate final

© Riley Sports Photography

HSBC World Rugby Sevens Series – selection panel of men and women referees: (L–R) Paddy O'Brien, Craig Joubert, myself, Alhambra Nievas, Anthony Moyles and Clare Daniels

Record breaker – making a presentation on behalf of World Rugby to Nigel Owens, in Fiji, ahead of him breaking the record for the number of international matches refereed

World Rugby – representing World Rugby on the eve of the World Rugby Sevens in Paris, 2019

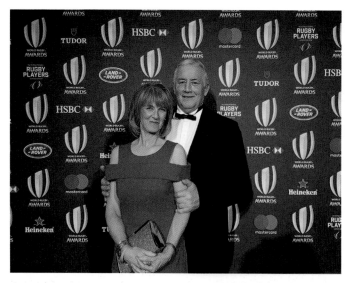

Treating the wife – me and Alana on our visit to Monaco for World Rugby's Players' Presentation Evening

The other Geraint Thomas – meeting 'G' at the World Rugby awards (my co-writer wishes to point out that he had the name first but is slower on a bike!)

© World Rugby

World Rugby Council, Japan 2019

© World Rugby

Referees' team building prior to RWC, Japan 2019

Preparing to take the plunge – (L–R) Rhys, Me, Tracy, Mark and Alain

Coming clean – cleansing ourselves beneath a mountain waterfall in Japan

Tbilisi – John Jeffrey, me, Mark Egan, and George from Georgia, Under-20s championship

Top ref – presenting Wayne Barnes with his referee of the year award following the RWC in Japan

© World Rugby

The next generation – my grandchildren Otis and Fletcher keeping the tradition going with both sports

disappointment that season having missed a November Test match against the United States of America, but that was down to my own stupidity – I had gotten myself sent off in a club game a few weeks before.

We were playing against Bridgend and I found myself on the receiving end of a sucker punch from their second row, Adrian Owen. It was not uncommon – if players had a chance they would stick one on you. We went down for a scrum and a punch came through, which split my eye. Our physio, Dai Jenkins, came on and told me I needed to be stitched up, but I was so annoyed I said, 'Do it at half-time!' It turned out that there would be plenty of time to see to my eye because soon after I went into a ruck and was hit from behind by the same player.

I turned and saw him running away after the ball, which had gone out, and gave chase. When I caught him up, I gave him the best left-hook I had. It was near to the players' tunnel and the referee, Les Peard, said to me, 'Don't bother stopping. Keep going down that tunnel.'

Adrian claimed afterwards that it was an accident, but, when I saw it on television the next day, I knew it was a deliberate act.

The ban really hurt as I had been more or less told that, with the USA over on tour, I was nailed for another cap. But all that changed when I was banned for eight weeks. The most disappointing thing about the whole episode was the USA were also playing against my county team, Brecknockshire, and I had to miss that one as well – and Brecknockshire beat them 15–9. What an occasion that would have been to be part of!

*

After the World Cup I felt that I had done enough to convince the selectors that I was worth persevering with, that I had the ability to make a real contribution to the team. I felt that I had improved with each international game I had played.

International rugby is an immensely pressurised and emotional event which some people come to terms with, and others do not. I wouldn't say that I failed to get to grips with it but there is always room for improvement. I was still learning the game at international level – it's a different animal to club rugby, it's three or four levels above that. Your heart rate is huge, you are outside your comfort zone. The whole emotion of it all took you to another level. I never quite felt that I had established myself as good enough to be the number one choice, although I genuinely felt I was in the top three loose-heads in Wales. But, like the club game, there was always someone coming up looking to take your place, just as I was trying to take someone else's position.

To say being left out was all one big anticlimax is an understatement. But, as disappointing as it was, you have to say to yourself, 'that's just how it is' and get on with things. There was no feedback, there never was in those days. The whole Welsh set-up was nothing like it is today. You didn't have the support staff, all the physios, coaches and psychologists. It was just a couple of hours training together a couple of times a week. It was very much an amateur situation.

As it turned out the selectors had picked a winning team, as two tries by Adrian Hadley helped Wales to a 3–11 win at Twickenham.

*

I put my disappointment behind me once more and went back to work underground. I still attended training sessions but was again overlooked when they named the side for the second fixture, at home to Scotland. The game was a classic, with Wales winning 25–20 thanks to two wonderful tries by Jonathan Davies and Ieuan Evans – two Llanelli boys! Ieuan's try saw the wonderful Scottish commentator, the much-missed Bill McLaren, labelling him 'Merlin the Magician'.

Ieuan was quite a character. You knew that he was something special, but he was never a great trainer in his early days – we used to have some fun around that – but if you put the ball in his hands, he was just electric. For me, he was one of the greatest players of my era. He was a finisher, a world-class try scorer. He was top end.

*

There was a real feeling of optimism around the Wales team going into the next game, against Ireland in Dublin, as we were in with a chance of a Triple Crown – awarded to the team that beat all three of the other home nations in the same season – for the first time since the golden years of Gareth Edwards and Co.

My hopes were raised when I was summoned to training with Wales on the Monday, but they were soon dashed when they announced the team and Staff was named. My good friend Phil May, who had been capped against England (I was really pleased for him – Laurance Delaney would go on to win his first cap the following season – as we had come through together in the pack when Gareth Jenkins had set about building his Llanelli side) tried to console me on the car journey home from training, saying, 'Don't worry, a lot can happen in a week.' Those words turned out to be prophetic!

News then reached me that Staff had injured his calf and that I might be playing after all! That led to a tense, emotional few days where I wondered, 'will I or won't I?' But the speculation ended when Staff passed his fitness test. It was a case of back to work once more, where I took a lot of stick from the boys who took great delight in saying, 'Buy a ticket like the rest of us!' People are only too happy to pat you on the back when you have been picked, but equally happy to have a go at you when you are dropped.

A large group of around 70 Ystradgynlais boys from the rugby club were going over to Dublin for the weekend but I couldn't join them as I had left it too late to book my place. However, opportunity comes along sometimes when you least expect it.

On the Thursday before the game I was back at work underground repairing a pump when my name was called on the tannoy system (everyone in the colliery can hear what is being said). I spoke to the control room and was told that somebody from the Welsh Rugby Union was on the telephone and wanted to speak to me. As you can imagine, everyone listening started giving me some good-natured ribbing, shouting, 'Get a ticket, Buchanan!'

My immediate reaction was that someone was playing a joke on me here, so I said, 'Don't take the p*** or I will come up there and see you.'

Viv in the control room replied, 'I'm dead serious. Get to a telephone.'

I got to one of the telephones underground and it was true, it was one of the secretaries from the Welsh Rugby Union. She said, 'You're in the team to play against Ireland. Can you get yourself to Cardiff Airport by 3 o'clock this afternoon?' This was at 11 o'clock in the morning.

Now I would never laugh at someone else's misfortune, but Staff had gone to stretch his leg and raised it on to one of the barriers around the national ground and pulled a hamstring in his hitherto uninjured leg. You couldn't make it up!

I arranged for someone to come down and take me back to the surface. As I made my way through the washery it was a bit like Roy of the Rovers, with everyone shouting and clapping. It was a wonderfully exciting moment that I will never forget.

I believe that I was the last working miner to play for Wales

– Garin Jenkins was also a miner but he had changed jobs at this time – which is quite an honour when you think of how the industry once dominated south Wales and provided so many players.

I made my way to the lamp room, where you are booked in and out of the mine, and was approached by the lampman, Gary. He said, 'Look, before you go, you must go up and see the manager.'

'You can tell the manager to F-off, I haven't got time! I've got to be at Cardiff Airport by 3 o'clock. And I have to go home and pack first.'

'Now listen to me,' he said firmly. 'Do yourself a favour and go and see the manager before you leave.'

I had a shower and changed. My heart was beating like mad with the excitement and I ran upstairs to the big office. I knocked on the door and it was opened by the manager, Mr Jones. He looked at me with a sort of relief on his face and said, 'Come in.'

I replied, 'Mr Jones, I really am pushed for time.' He just turned and so I followed him into his office. Inside, sat at the large oak table, were three very important, dour-looking gentlemen who, as it turned out, were mine inspectors. Mr Jones gestured towards me and declared proudly, 'Gentlemen, this is Anthony Buchanan. He has just been selected to play for Wales against Ireland on Saturday in the Triple Crown match!'

The three gentlemen looked at me and said half-heartedly, 'All the best.' I turned and started walking towards the door when Mr Jones pulled me back and whispered, 'No stay, don't go.'

These inspectors were from Yorkshire. They had no interest in rugby; they were there to inspect the mine. Mr Jones must have been under pressure because he was trying to change the subject and talk about me, which they weren't having. It was quite farcical. I was trying to get out of the door and he was holding on to me. 'Just give me five minutes,' he begged in my ear.

This also reminds me of a moment regarding Mr Jones on my return from the World Cup. I had a phone call from the colliery secretary telling me that Mr Jones wanted to present me with a watch before the day shift on Friday. I turned up at 7 o'clock to find that all the day shift were in the canteen waiting for the presentation. As you can imagine, this didn't go down well with the men who were eager to get underground and earn money. I could feel the emotion of everyone in the room, and several comments were made, like, 'Just give him the bloody watch!' An uncomfortable presentation.

As I was driving home, I detoured to pick Alana up from school. She was teaching at Maesydderwen and I would have to go and get her first to pack for me. As I ran into the school, I couldn't help but smile when I thought of my old PE teacher, Gareth Thomas, who had given me the 'dap' when I refused to play rugby all those years ago, and yet, here I was, about to play for Wales.

We had long since 'made up', as it were. He was a lovely person, along with his wife Ann. Often in life, when you come across people you encounter them later again; he was a real gent. Being a former All Whites player and myself playing for Llanelli, it was like a red flag to a bull and we often crossed swords good-naturedly. Whether Gareth thought I would have been an even better player had I played at school, I will never know, but he did say to me once, 'You should have gone to the All Whites. You would have won more caps if you had!'

After my first Welsh cap the school recognised the fact and invited me back a few times for presentations or to speak to the pupils. It's still a huge honour for a school to have just one person go on and represent their country in sport, and it's a heck of an achievement for Maesydderwen to have had myself, Alun Donovan, Kevin Hopkins, Huw

Richards and, more recently, Adam Jones, achieve that in rugby.

I found Alana in the middle of a lesson. I knocked on the door and she hurried out and said, 'What's the matter?'

'I've been picked to play on Saturday,' I said.

'Give me a minute and I will get someone to cover me and come home with you.'

You may think I was useless not being able to pack on my own, but there is so much involved. You must have your tuxedo, your dickie bow tie, all the Welsh gear, the whole shooting match. It was a mad rush but we got everything packed, although it wasn't until I arrived in Dublin that I realised I had brought everything – apart from pants and socks!

I finally made it to Cardiff where I faced a barrage of questions from media crews before joining the squad for the short flight across the Irish Sea.

When you are a player, on the Friday you get a limited number of tickets for the game. After our morning training session, I took mine over to the hotel where the Ystradgynlais boys were staying, to give my allocation to my brother-in-law Kevin and some of the boys.

After your team run-out on the Friday morning, you then try to relax for the rest of the day. Traditionally you go to the cinema in the evening. When I was at the hotel my mother phoned me to say, as my father wasn't well enough to travel, my Uncle Peter was coming over on his own, and could I get him a ticket? My uncle was a lovely man. He was an All-Whites supporter but, despite that, he always supported me whenever I played. I was dismayed and said, 'I've given all my tickets away.' Remember, this was the Triple Crown match, the first in almost a decade, and tickets were as rare as rocking horse manure.

This was playing on my mind. I felt terrible, and I couldn't concentrate on the film. Then I realised that the Ystradgynlais boys were in a hotel just around the corner from where we were and, as we were leaving the cinema at around 10 o'clock, I asked Derek Quinnell if I could have a word.

I said, 'Look, I'm in desperate need of a ticket for my uncle and I've asked everyone and there are none spare. Do you mind if I just nip to the hotel and get one of my tickets back from my mates?' Fortunately, he said yes and told me to make it quick.

Now, I didn't really think this through. It was late at night, on the eve of a massive international, and the supporters had been out drinking all day. Can you imagine the scene as I walked into the hotel? The vast majority of the supporters couldn't say bread, they were so intoxicated, and there's me asking for a ticket. All I can say is that the experience of seeing Welsh supporters out on a Friday night in Dublin is something I will never forget.

As soon as I was spotted, I faced a barrage of questions. 'Buchanan, what the hell are you doing out at this time of night?'

'Don't you dare let us down tomorrow!'

I explained I was looking for a ticket I had.

'Why do you need a ticket? You're playing!'

I soon realised that I was never going to get any sense from anybody in there. It was absolutely pointless. Anyone who has been with people who are drunk while you are stone cold sober will know how I felt – you see the most ridiculous things and hear absolute rubbish.

I decided to leave but, as I approached the door, one supporter, who could hardly stand, decided to punch me on the arm and tell me not to let them down tomorrow.

'No problem,' I said, and I tried to walk away but he followed me and punched me again. I made the mistake of turning around and saying to him, 'If you punch me again I will drop you.'

'You wanna fight, do you?' he declared. 'Come on then!'

And he started taking his coat off. I thought to myself, the

Wales team are outside waiting for me. I'm playing against Ireland tomorrow. This guy wants to fight me, and I haven't got a ticket for my uncle. What am I going to do?

I left and climbed on the bus and went back to the hotel with the team. I was worried sick because I realised, come Saturday morning, getting any ticket would be out of my range. All my focus would have to be on the game. I felt terrible because I knew how much of an effort my uncle had made to come over to support me.

Once back at the hotel I sat down with Phil May. I was particularly close to Phil and he was always great company and a fantastic captain to play under. I could never make out how, for someone who always put his body on the line, he never seemed to pick up cuts on his bald head when he always had cuts everywhere else!

I said to Phil, 'I don't know what I'm going to do. This is really starting to affect me now. It's taking my thoughts away from the game.'

Phil turned to me and said, 'Go and see the Big Five and tell them your problem.'

I decided to take his advice, but I failed to take into account, once again, that it was 11 o'clock on a Friday night in Dublin before an international game.

I steeled myself and went upstairs to the room where I knew they were and knocked on the door. John Dawes opened the door in a cloud of cigarette smoke and the smell of whiskey. Now John was a nice guy and he said to me, 'What's the matter?'

'I need a ticket,' I replied.

Once again, I was greeted with, 'Why do you want a ticket? You're playing.'

'My uncle is travelling from Wales overnight and I can't let him travel without getting him a ticket. Whatever it takes, I have to find a ticket for him. I want to start focusing on the game and my head is all over the place.'

He disappeared into the smoke and returned a few minutes later with a ticket. I have seldom felt so relieved. The next morning I took the ticket down to reception and left it in an envelope for my uncle to collect – finally I could turn my attention to the game.

*

The game itself was a brilliant occasion, although international matches, as all players will tell you, really do pass you in a blur. I can remember running out of the tunnel onto the pitch in the old Lansdowne Road stadium and looking straight across into the crowd and seeing Robert Davies who ran the chemist shop in Ystradgynlais. I remember seeing him in a crowd of nearly 50,000, right there on the halfway line. It settled me a little as I knew then where the boys were in the stand. All the same, I was very nervous. It was a huge occasion and Ireland were a tough bunch.

I was up against my old mate Des Fitzgerald, who I had first locked horns with on my first away trip with Llanelli. I wasn't intimidated by Des – I had also played alongside him for the Barbarians – and we had become quite pally. It was the same with the rest of their front five. I had faced them all before.

Much like the game against England in the World Cup, it wasn't a classic by any means, but the most important statistic was the final score, 9–12. We won! Paul Thorburn, who had also been recalled to the team, won the game at the death with one of his kicks – just as he had done against Australia in the third-place play-off.

It was a phenomenal feeling to be involved in winning a Triple Crown – a mixture of relief and emotion. The pride in what you had achieved would settle in later and last a lifetime.

When you played out in Dublin you always knew that, whoever won, you would have a good craic with the Irish boys after the game – and that was certainly the case that night. I was pleased because I had scrummaged particularly well – so much so that, after the game, Des Fitzgerald started giving me some advice for the final game against the French, but I told him that I had a feeling I wouldn't be in the team. He couldn't believe it and said, 'You gave me a really tough time today, I can't see them not picking you.'

Noel Murphy, an Irish rugby legend, said to me after the game, 'I've seen Des play hundreds of times and you really gave him a tough time, which is rare.'

Sure enough, when the team was announced a few days later, I was dropped, and Staff Jones was back in – I wasn't even named on the bench. I remember thinking it was rare for someone to recover from a hamstring in less than a week!

This time I was heartbroken to be honest. So much so in fact that when they invited me along to Cardiff for the game so that I could be part of the set-up, I declined, telling them I had a family wedding, which was true, but it was a distant relative and I could have made my excuses. You could say that there was a touch of sour grapes on my part, but I honestly felt I had done enough against Ireland to retain my place. It wasn't a great game, in fact it was bloody lousy, but our scrum had gone well, and we had won. It would be another 17 years before Wales won a Triple Crown again.

I did find a television to watch the game, and I genuinely wanted the boys to win – they were my mates after all. It was obviously an even bigger occasion than the Triple Crown game, with the Grand Slam (when a side wins all their matches in the championship) at stake, something Wales hadn't achieved since 1978.

The French, who had lost earlier in the tournament to Scotland, were good to be fair to them, and it was a tight game that eventually broke Welsh hearts as we lost 9–10. I took no comfort in the result.

*

Once again, what had ultimately been a disappointing international season for myself – albeit with a major high out in Dublin – finished on a high as I was named in the Wales squad to tour New Zealand.

There were a number of Llanelli boys in the squad – seven in all, plus Gary Jones flew out as a replacement later on – which was a great testament to what Gareth Jenkins had built at Stradey Park.

On the club front Llanelli enjoyed another great season and we found ourselves in the Schweppes Cup final, against Neath once more. It meant that I played the game on the Saturday and was due to fly out to New Zealand on the Monday. In truth, I should never have gone as during the last five minutes of the Cup final my head went to the ground, the scrum drove over me, and I felt something click in my neck. I felt quite sore after the game and took some advice from a few of the boys and they all said, 'Don't say anything, just get on the plane.'

I faced a similar dilemma to the one I faced when deciding to own up to my breathing problems before the South Seas tour. Fortunately, by the Sunday evening, it felt a little better and I travelled genuinely believing that I was OK.

I was selected in the side to play the second game, against Wellington, and when I hit a scrum I lost the use of my left arm – it went very weak. Rather foolishly, especially in hindsight, I didn't tell anyone and continued to play.

While I was in Wellington I was invited out for an evening meal with Dick Evans, chairman of the New Zealand supporters' club, and his wife, because I had won the Wellington trophy for Llanelli RFC Sportsman of the Year 1987, awarded by the supporters of the club. During the meal we started chatting about his time travelling with the New Zealand team and their supporters. To my amazement, he started to mention his time in Wales and also the Gwalia Hotel in London, mentioning Susan and Hugh who I was very friendly with and lived in Ystradgynlais – isn't this a small world?

I wasn't involved in the first Test; they had stuck with Staff Jones, and while the casual observer would say that was a good thing – as Wales were given another hiding, 52–3, by the rampant All Blacks – it still hurt.

There were three more provincial games before the second Test and I was determined to give it everything I had to make the starting line-up, especially as the Big Five must have been contemplating changes following such a poor performance in the first Test. However, my neck problem had not gone away. We were scrummaging every day in training and eventually I felt that there really was something wrong.

Things came to a head after I sought out our rub-a-dub man – who gave us a rub down to ease sore muscles. He was a New Zealander who had been assigned to us and we had become quite friendly; he was a good man. He was working the top of my shoulders when he said, 'We've got a problem here.'

I replied, 'I know, I've had it for a while. I lose the strength in my left arm.'

'We can't have this,' he said, and he called the physios in, who in turn summoned Rod Morgan, the chairman of selectors, and said, 'This player needs an X-ray.'

I was sent off to the hospital and X-rayed in every position possible. They discovered that when I was hitting the scrum hard, the pressure was closing the vertebrates on to a nerve, and I was losing all the strength in my arm. They stretched me like a rubber doll and gave me some traction and it eased somewhat.

I thought the problem had been cured but, a while later, there was a knock on my door and Rod Morgan came in and said we needed to sit down and talk. Then he dropped the bombshell and said, 'I don't want to select you again on tour. This tour has gone; we're dead on our feet and the risk to your health is just not worth it.'

I wasn't happy. We were already down to the bare bones – the rugby was brutal, and we were dropping like flies and I didn't want to be the next one. I think the tour set a new record for the number of replacements who had to be flown out – it almost seemed as if the bus driver would be asked to play by the end!

'I don't want to go home,' I told him. 'Can't I have treatment?' I begged. 'If there's any chance of me being able to play, I want to stay.' There was no way I was going to throw in the towel, there was no way I was going home. But I didn't want to prevent anybody else having a chance. The management reluctantly agreed, and I was told that they weren't going to fly anyone out because there were only two games remaining.

That evening I rang home and Alana said, 'You're coming home.'

'What do you mean?'

'It's all over the news,' she replied. Someone must have leaked the information as the headlines on the back pages were, 'Buchanan the latest to fly home'.

'No I'm not,' I said. 'I'm staying.'

'You can't stay, you're injured.'

'I'm having treatment and I believe I can possibly make the last Test.'

I had been roomed with the Neath hooker Kevin Phillips ahead of the last Test and, placing a prop and a hooker together, saw us both jump to the conclusion that we were about to be selected to play. When they announced the team, and we had both been overlooked, Kevin was climbing the walls. He went absolutely ape.

I was so disappointed, but Rod Morgan sat me down once more and said, 'Look Bucks, there's no way we're taking you home on a stretcher.' I could understand their position and, of course, I had no choice but to accept it.

Eventually, I needed an operation to repair the damage to the discs in my neck. I was very fortunate in that I had a good friend, John Martin, who was a neurosurgeon and he told me he would do this once I had finished playing.

The second Test proved to be just as dire as the first and we were hammered 54–9, although Jonathan Davies showed his class by scoring a brilliant length of the field, individual try.

*

We played eight games and lost six, including the two Tests. A lot has been written on the subject over the years but the best way of describing it was we were like a car that had run out of petrol, or in a boxing match and we were on the ropes in the ninth round. We were drained. Whoever made the decision to return to New Zealand, so soon after the World Cup, needed their head examined. You can't say it was a suicide mission, but it was pretty close to one.

We had toured three years on the trot – the South Seas, the World Cup and now, probably the hardest challenge of them all, we found ourselves in New Zealand. To me it was a tour too far. It came off the back of a long, hard domestic season of 30 to 35 games and we were a tired team. And to go back to New Zealand, after they had just won the World Cup and were on a high, was an unbelievably tough task.

The team had been really challenged. It was really competitive rugby which often bordered on brutal – the raking and the kicking you had was unbelievable. My back was torn to pieces. It was tough on me but I wasn't alone. Jonathan Mason, the Pontypridd fullback, had just got married and was on honeymoon with his new wife in Majorca. They were lying on the beach when his wife said to Jonathan, 'There's someone over there holding a sign up with your name on it.'

He looked up and, sure enough, someone was paging him. He identified himself and was told to contact the Welsh Rugby Union immediately. He went back to the hotel and found a phone and discovered he had been called up as a replacement and they arranged to fly him out to New Zealand that day.

He was thrown right in the deep end and selected to face North Auckland. Their outside-half put up this huge up-and-under and, by the time Jonathan caught it, the whole pack had descended upon him like a herd of wild buffalo. They raked and stamped all over him and even dragged him down the field for about five metres before scoring a try under the posts. As we were waiting for the conversion, I looked at him and his shirt and shorts were in rags and he had stud marks all over his back. After the game he said to me, 'I wish I had just buried my head in the sand and stayed on honeymoon!' The pain was worth it in the end because he was on the bench for the second Test and came on to earn his cap.

I don't think anyone would have come close to the All Blacks at that point in time – they were so far ahead of the rest of us. When we were over there we saw a lot of the All Blacks on television adverts – it was taken up by the IRB. We realised that they were more or less professional players. They had jobs but their employers would allow them to do daytime training. We realised that they were getting away from us with regard to their fitness. They were streets ahead. They also had tremendous team spirit – they were very close as a group of players and were known as 'the Club'. The All Blacks had so many fixtures, they were like a club side. I think that was their strength.

*

The fall-out following the tour was horrendous – the inquests into what had gone wrong raged on and on in every workplace, bar and rugby club across Wales. Tony Gray and Derek

Quinnell were basically sacked and replaced by John Ryan, but the most damaging aftershock was Wales basically lost a whole team of stars to rugby league.

I can't say, had we been successful in New Zealand then the boys would have turned down the opportunity to go North – I do think that the money and lifestyle it brought was the main driver – but it must have been a factor.

Jonathan Davies was probably the biggest loss and his move shocked Welsh rugby. I remember Llanelli played a game over Christmas and the rumours were flying around that he was going North. He told the boys in the changing rooms after the game that he wasn't going as there wasn't enough money in it for him.

I went back to Ystrad Rugby Club later and everyone was screaming that they didn't want him to go, so I said, 'Boys, he's not going.'

The headlines the next day were, 'Davies goes North'.

When I saw him next I said, 'I thought you weren't going.'

'They offered me more money,' he said.

He proved himself a world-class player by reaching the top in both codes of rugby. He was an all-round sportsman but, not only that, he was a good person as well. He was comical, he was talented, and he was good for the team. He didn't have a big ego about him.

At that moment in time it seemed like one of our rugby stars headed North each day. Wales was pillaged by rugby league and it did so much damage to the Welsh team, losing the likes of Jonathan, John Devereux, Paul Moriarty, Dai Young, Alan Bateman, Adrian Hadley, my pal Stuart Evans, and Rowland Phillips. It was a major blow to Welsh rugby and exposed us to difficult times. They were quality players we could ill afford to lose. It was sad. We had finished third in the Rugby World Cup, had just won a Triple Crown and finished top of the Five Nations table, and yet we were back to rebuilding a team from scratch.

As for myself, I did receive some attention from rugby league, but it wasn't something that ever interested me. I never saw myself going somewhere else to live – I was too much of a home bird. Perhaps the game would have suited me, as I was a little bit of a loose forward, and I think that it's a great game to watch. My wife's uncle, Les Anthony, left the colliery and went north to Oldham and played for Wales, so it was in the family.

CHAPTER 9

Hanging Up My Boots

DESPITE HELPING WALES to a Triple Crown and touring New Zealand, I found myself out of favour the following season – I wasn't even invited to the Wales trials. Mike Griffiths, the Bridgend prop, came to the fore and I think they realised that they wanted to develop younger players. I knew that it was coming, that my time in the sun was running out, but I had come to the end of three years of tremendous opportunities which, hand on heart, I never dreamed would have come my way.

When I first played for Wales everyone thought I had played rugby as a youngster – they didn't realise I hadn't taken up the game until relatively late in life. Then came the realisation that I wasn't as young as they thought I was – I was into my thirties and I suppose that played a part in the thought process of the Big Five.

I still had the hunger to play for Llanelli, but I did experience a bit of a drop in form – it had been an exhausting three years of non-stop rugby and it had taken its toll on me. It was hardly surprising – we had had the crap kicked out of us in New Zealand, yet two weeks later we were into the new season. I was also still struggling with my neck, especially when making contact in the scrums, and it did cross my mind that I could do some serious damage to myself, and that knocked my confidence. I also lost a bit of interest if I'm being honest.

Matters came to a head when I was dropped to play

against Cardiff in the Cup. When the team was announced, Alan Phillips, the Cardiff hooker, phoned me up and said he couldn't believe I had been left out of the team. I remember going home disappointed, especially as New Zealand were over on tour and due to play Llanelli soon. Alana said to me, 'Well, you're not running any more. You never go out for a run on Sunday nights.' I realised that I had let myself slip and I had to get my fitness back. I had to find my mojo again.

Fortunately, I managed to pull my finger out and win my place back as first-choice loose-head in the Llanelli side, and was selected to play against the All Blacks. As I have recounted earlier in the book, the game was played in hurricane conditions and I am sure that, had it not been a touring All Blacks team, the game would have been called off. The game was lost 0–11 and they then went on to beat Wales.

As it turned out, we fared far better against the All Blacks. Wales, once again, were well beaten in Cardiff, 9–34. The result heaped further pressure on the Wales coach, John Ryan, and he was replaced by Ron Waldron who, at the time, was a popular choice inasmuch as Neath were one of the dominating sides in British rugby.

Towards the end of the season, to my surprise, Ron phoned me up and asked whether I would consider a return to the international fold – not that I had ever announced my retirement! Wales were due to tour Namibia and he wanted 'an old head' to help the team develop. I was obviously flattered and seriously tempted, as I believed I still had something to offer, but I suppose I chose to listen to my head over my heart.

From what I could work out, Namibia was a one-horse town, and I knew that there were a number of young players coming through, so I wouldn't even be second choice, and I didn't feel like hanging around on the sidelines. I thanked him but said that it wasn't for me, and wished him all the best. I knew deep down, conscious of the fact that I was approaching 36, it was the right decision and I had no regrets.

There was, however, another opportunity to tour, as Llanelli were going to California at the same time. We had quite a large beer kitty which, as a senior player, I was in charge of! I wanted the Californian tour to be my swansong because I knew my retirement from the club game was just around the corner. I wanted to finish off my career with the boys who I had developed alongside, players such as Phil May, Laurance Delaney, Dai Fox, Nigel Davies and Phil Davies. It proved to be the right decision as it was by far the best tour I ever went on.

I have so many fantastic memories and, as the old saying goes, 'What happens on tour stays on tour', but I will share a couple of the more hilarious stories with you here. Sean Gale and I were the signatories for the beer kitty. Shortly after arriving at our hotel we went out to cash some cheques for quite a considerable amount of money, and found ourselves in a bank near to where the trams turned around in San Francisco. We proceeded to the counter and produced the paperwork but were informed that they only had $20 bills available. Sean and I were dressed in shorts and T-shirts, and when the cashier produced six-and-a-half thousand dollars in $20 bills, it was quite a wad I can tell you.

Not wanting to walk the mean streets with such a magnet for thieves, the only place that I could put it was down my shorts. Telling Sean to watch my back, as I would probably be able to manage anything that came from my front, we set off.

On the way back we also had to pick up something to give as a presentation to the tour manager, secretary and officials. We proceeded to a glassware shop where there were decanters and crystal bowls and such like. After placing our order, the lady behind the counter turned around and, looking at my crotch, said, 'I have got to tell you, you are either well gifted or a shoplifter.'

I replied, 'If you gift wrap what I've just ordered, I'll show you what I've got!'

On producing six-and-a-half thousand dollars' worth of $20 bills from out of the front of my shorts, the lady was absolutely blown away! She would not let us leave the shop until she had a taxi waiting outside to take us straight back to the hotel, because she said that she didn't feel that we would make it back alive on foot.

On another occasion we had been given the day off from training and ended up going to a very picturesque harbour. Some of us decided to just chill out on some sun loungers, while the more adventurous looked for something to do.

Phil Davies, Gareth Jenkins, Laurance Delaney and I decided to hire a small speedboat. With the rest of the boys watching, we set off from the jetty with myself in charge at the back, steering the boat.

It didn't take long for Laurance to decide that he was far more experienced at the helm, as he owned his own fishing boat, and he wanted to take over.

As Laurance and I were changing positions the throttle was knocked off sending the front of the boat into a dive. To counteract it Laurance proceeded to pull the throttle to full on, which sent the boat into a submarine dive resulting in it doing a complete flip sending the four of us into the water. I believe Gareth and Phil were actually under the boat while Laurance and I were thrown clear. It was a frightening experience as the only way you could tell which was up or down was by the colour of a light or dark blue. We were rescued by the harbour patrol which towed us back into the quay where I had hired the boat from. In fairness, they were more concerned with our safety rather than the damage to the boat.

*

The tour was brilliant, but I also received some devastating news whilst away that was to change my life tremendously (although I didn't know it at the time) for the better.

I telephoned home to check in with Alana and she told me that she had some bad news.

'What is it?' I asked, imagining all sorts.

'They've closed Blaenant down,' she said. 'You will have to come back home, you're out of work.'

'But I'm in charge of the beer kitty,' I replied, not really grasping the seriousness of the situation.

After hanging up I called the agent who was handling the closure of the mine and discovered it was indeed true. They had basically decided to close with immediate effect, and it had closed overnight. I was told I had a decision to make – whether to take redundancy or transfer to Tower Colliery near Hirwaun. I knew if I went to Tower all the good jobs would have already been taken, and I would end up doing something like cleaning the belts, which didn't appeal to me one bit.

Unlike most of the boys, I was kept on for six to eight weeks as a contractor tasked with stripping the mine of anything that could be salvaged before it was sealed up. It was so sad to see – the whole place had been ransacked, and all my tools had been stolen along with anything else they could carry.

History tells us it was just a part of the terminal decline of the once great coal industry, but at the time it was a hell of a blow, not just to the men who worked there but their families and communities – it was devastating. I was fortunate in that Alana had a solid teaching job, but it was still a massive shock. I had spent 15 years working underground and made countless friends. The place had fond memories for me, but it was erased from existence – there isn't even a plaque there today, it has all gone.

When I came off the phone Gareth saw the look on my face and asked, 'What's the matter?'

'I've lost my job,' I replied, devastated.

'So come and work with me,' he replied, matter-of-factly.

I said, 'I don't know anything about chemicals.' Gareth ran a chemical and water treatment company called Quasar.

'You can learn,' he replied.

I made a decision there, and then telephoned Alana back and said that I was taking redundancy and going to work with Gareth. I will always be grateful for that opportunity.

*

Gareth was an outstanding coach and his legacy with Llanelli and the Scarlets will stand the test of time. It is such a shame that he wasn't allowed to have more time with the national side, having been discarded following a disappointing exit from the 2007 World Cup. I genuinely believe he was treated harshly towards the end of his tenure in charge of the Wales team. Quite a few of the Welsh players still playing today – Alun Wyn Jones and Jamie Roberts – were given their opportunities by Gareth. Unfortunately for Gareth, his team delivered for other coaches.

*

On my return from America, I found myself sat in an office, with a collar and tie, learning a new job. I was basically a sales rep, and my patch was east Wales. Gareth was sales director and he had west Wales. What hit home to me was that I would go into places and say, 'Anthony Buchanan from Quasar,' and I could see the cogs in their minds ticking over.

'Do you play for the Scarlets?' they would ask. Then I would spend an hour talking about rugby before they would ask what I do. Then they would ask technical questions and I would say, 'I have no idea, but I will get somebody to talk to you who knows all the answers.'

The banter was always great. One of my calls was at TRW

Automotive Holdings Corp in the Neath Valley where 90 per cent were Neath supporters, and the joke was that I would enter the front door if Llanelli had won and the back door if we had lost!

I increased the company's turnover significantly and rugby played a huge part in that. If I was called Jones or Williams I doubt I would have made any headway, but as soon as I mentioned Buchanan the link with rugby clicked and it opened doors. You could have selected an international team made up of chemical reps at that time, with the likes of Paul Turner, Phil Bennett, Bobby Windsor, Steve Fenwick, Tommy David and Derek Quinnell all involved with chemicals and water treatment.

*

Even when my rugby playing days came to an end, Gareth did it in such a way that made me make the final decision and allowed me to find a new path on my rugby journey into management. He approached me at the start of the following season, 1990/91, and broached a subject which I knew in my heart of hearts was unavoidable – my retirement. Phil Davies was captain at the time, and he was keen for me to stay on as first choice, but Gareth was looking to the future. He said, 'Look, we're going to have to give Ricky Evans rugby if we're going to find out if he's up to it, and you'll be disappointed not to be picked if you still believe you are first choice. We have to rebuild and there's you, Laurance Delaney, Russell Cornelius – you are all getting on and I have to start replacing you one at a time. You are the oldest and you're the one we're going to replace first.' Australia were due to tour the following year and they wanted a settled side in place.

In fairness he added, 'It's your choice. You probably could be the number one for the season, but the reality is we need to bring Ricky in.'

I went home and discussed it with Alana and came to the conclusion that I never wanted to be in a situation where I received a 'Dear John' letter saying thanks for your service but we no longer require you. I decided to take the option of calling time myself. That was always something I wanted to do.

I had for quite a while thought about going into coaching after hanging up my boots, and had started preparing for it. Whilst in New Zealand, I spoke to a lot of people and brought as much literature on the subject as possible home with me. I discussed my desire to get into coaching with Gareth and he invited me to take over the youth team at Llanelli. It was an exciting time, with a certain young Scott Quinnell coming through the ranks. You just couldn't believe it when Scott played, it was a different team. You could see the potential in him becoming an international, British Lion and a world-class player. He was just head and shoulders above everyone else. When Scott played, the team did well. He was a terrific leader and rugby player, even at that age.

It was a strange feeling turning up at Stradey and not playing. One of my first games in charge was on the second-team pitch at the same time as Llanelli were playing at home. Some supporters spotted me and they shouted out, 'What are you doing out there, Buchanan? Get back in here and play!'

*

One of my regular contacts in my day job was a firm in Pontypool called Parke-Davis Pharmaceutical. Quite naturally, they were all big Pooler supporters. I was there on a Wednesday and they were all rubbing their hands ahead of a home game against Llanelli on the Saturday. We had a lot of banter about the game and I told them that the Scarlets would do the business. They were good people, they looked after me and treated me well business-wise, despite the fact I was a

Turk, as Llanelli people are called. Bobby Windsor, the Wales and Pontypool legend, was trying to get in there, chasing the business, and he would say, 'Why have you got that Turk in here?' To be fair they replied, 'Listen, until he lets us down, we will deal with him.'

I turned up to coach the youth team on the Thursday and someone shouted over the wall for me to go to the first team's changing rooms. I went to see what they wanted, and Gareth sat me down and said, 'We have a problem. Ricky Evans is not available and Sean Gale is injured, and we have no loose-head for Saturday. Would you be prepared to help us out in Pontypool?'

'Of course,' I replied without a second's hesitation.

Pontypool away from home was an experience that quite a number of senior players avoided at all costs! You would be waiting for the bus and players would be pulling out left, right and centre. Personally, I always enjoyed playing at Pontypool Park, but it was the most formidable of places. They were renowned for having a grinding, mean-machine of a pack. The first thing that hit you was their support; it was amongst the most vocal around and they were as one-eyed as the Scarlet supporters! And then you had David Bishop kicking the ball up so high it was going outside the floodlights. Our back three had to be brave because by the time they caught it they had all of the Pontypool pack on top of them. It was not for the faint-hearted.

I went up there once with quite a young group of inexperienced boys. I gathered them around and said, 'Whatever happens, we will stick together. Don't try to get out of the scrum early.'

They knew we always used a Channel 1 ball, so the first scrum we had near their line we decided to keep the ball in and double shove them. All their back row had broken off, their second rows were starting to leave, and we had a pushover try. As it turned out, that was not a clever thing to do. We had dented their pride and after that we were mullered in every scrum!

Now, having agreed to help Gareth out, without any pre-season training whatsoever, I turned up in Pontypool and, much to the annoyance of the people at Parke-Davis Pharmaceutical, I scored the winning try! Phil Davis jumped on top of me, and Rupert Moon kissed me on the lips!

Scoring that try resulted in me not being allowed to go inside the Pooler supporting Parke-Davis Pharmaceutical again! Not because I had played but because I didn't tell them that I was playing. I tried to tell them that I'd had no idea that I was going to play.

*

I went on to help Llanelli out a further three times that season, with my last game in a scarlet jersey coming against Newbridge away. It was an emotional moment. My Llanelli career had spanned 226 games over ten seasons, and included 27 tries – not bad for a prop forward.

*

The 1990/91 season was highly significant in Welsh rugby, not because it was my swansong but because it saw the introduction of league rugby across our domestic game. Rugby was a huge participation sport at the time, the number of players was high, and there had been a growing clamour for change in the game, not least from junior clubs who longed for a seat at the top table. I want to go on record, however, as saying I honestly believe the Heineken League was the biggest disaster to hit Welsh rugby.

I used to call in at the club in Ystradgynlais for a pint and all the old boys would tell me it was only a matter of time before they were in the same league as Llanelli. I did my best to convince them that this was a road which would end in disaster – junior clubs just didn't have the support, infrastructure or history which surrounded clubs like Llanelli, Neath and Swansea.

I do not want to disrespect the clubs, but it led to a huge influx of cash into the grassroots game. There was a gold rush. It made people dream about being further up the league and ended up bankrupting a lot of clubs. You had a £10,000 bonus for winning your division, and so clubs gambled and brought players in and paid them – if they didn't get promoted they were in debt. I heard stories of players at the lower level being paid big salaries. It was unsustainable and it took years for clubs to recover financially.

Ystradgynlais eventually reached the second division, just one promotion away from playing Llanelli. But it nearly bankrupted them, and they went right back down to Division 5. I always felt that having first- and second-class clubs worked far better than everyone being in the same pot. It gave me no pleasure being proved correct.

CHAPTER 10

Team Manager

I WAS ONLY in the youth coaching role for a few months, partly because they called me back to the first team to cover for injuries, but mainly because I was offered what was, at the time, a revolutionary role in rugby, that of team manager.

Gareth Jenkins was very forward thinking, and he had established a rugby committee (separate from the rugby club) which oversaw the day-to-day off-field matters associated with running a club the size of Llanelli. It was tasked with making rugby decisions very quickly. They needed somebody on the rugby committee who the players respected and could relate to. As someone who was known to the players, having only just hung up my boots, they asked whether I was prepared to take on the role. They wanted to keep me involved with Llanelli and I suppose they saw me as dependable. I had learned a lot during my ten years down at Stradey and I shared the same rugby philosophy as Gareth, so it was a natural progression for me.

Previously you had a match secretary whose job it was to phone around the players, but the game was changing fast. With the advent of the Heineken League, and although it had not yet gone open, the game was becoming more and more professional in its practice and it was important to reflect that in the manner players were looked after. I was given responsibility for all matters off the field around the team. The role just grew on me. I managed the kit, ensured players met for training and games on time, handled their expenses and looked after their general welfare. You may recall I had grown up in football and had always been impressed with the way Cwm Rovers had been run by the committee, and I guess I had learned a lot from their values and approach to players.

Knowing that I was still keen on the coaching side of the game, Gareth also offered me the position of coaching the front row alongside that of team manager. I used all the information I had garnered in New Zealand and I had also learnt a lot from Gareth on how to play the game in the Llanelli way. It took up a lot of my time – I still had the day job – but I was fortunate that my family supported me. I was really enthused about still being in the game at this level.

I had mixed emotions when I began doing a bit of coaching as I still thought that I could play, although the reality was I could not. I took a great deal of pleasure in seeing players such as Sean Gale, Ricky Evans, Iestyn Thomas and Martyn Madden come through. I was able to pass on to them all that I had learnt through my own experiences. We had a hydraulic scrummaging machine which I used to fine tune the pack, and I would take sessions individually and speak to them about their technique. I would offer tips, like not offering their elbow and the correct placement of their head. These were things which I had learnt the hard way through experience. I honestly believe you cannot teach somebody how to scrummage, you can only give pointers they can then try in the game. If it works for them, fine; if it doesn't, they can try another method. You must find a tool to develop your scrummaging for yourself. It appeared to work as they all developed into great players. Best of all, I still felt part of the team, which was important to me.

*

As you can imagine, there were plenty of characters in the squad – Lyn Jones, Dai Joseph and Chris Wyatt top the list!

143

I had many sleepless nights trying to keep them all in order. With Heineken sponsoring the league, they used to give out awards – in the form of slabs of beer – each month depending on how well you were doing. I decided to store them away until the end of the season so we could all have a big party. They were locked away in a room in Stradey but I noticed that a few had gone missing – without wanting to name and shame I had my suspicions as to who the culprits were!

On the subject of drinking, we always stopped on the way home from away games for a few drinks. It was important as it built up team spirit. On one occasion we didn't have time to stop and the beer kitty – around £150 in notes – was in my bag and came home with me. Unfortunately, my dog got into the bag and chewed it all up. When I saw what he had done I gathered all the pieces together and put them in an envelope and gave them to our treasurer, who was also a bank manager. I explained what had happened and he said to leave it with him.

He phoned me up the following day and said, 'Right, I've managed to prove that there's £130, which we can replace, but that leaves us £20 short.'

'Well,' I replied, 'you will have to wait until the dog goes to the toilet for the rest.'

*

There were so many sides to the role. Anthony Copsey, our former second row, was appointed Commercial Manager and we were tasked with sorting a new kit out for the club. We set off for an appointment with Johnny Hamburger of Jenson Sports up in north-east England. As we were travelling in that direction, we called in to see Bill Newton, an old friend who had been working for Umbro but had since started a company called 'Kooga made for rugby', based in Rochdale. I gave him a call en route and fixed up a meeting. We were so impressed with what he had to offer that we signed a deal there and then – I think we were the first side to go with Kooga.

The kit was delivered to the club shop and attracted the attention of some of the players, which resulted in a few items going missing! If they thought they could outfox me, they had another thing coming. When it came to handing the kit out, the guilty parties complained that they hadn't been given a certain amount of kit.

I said, 'We both know that you've already had yours.'

While I was easygoing and still one of the boys, there was a line that I couldn't allow the players to cross. This became clear to me after an incident involving a visit from the drug testing team. Unfortunately, steroids had become a big issue in Welsh rugby during the '90s as players sought to get an edge. In order to clean up the game the WRU introduced regular drug tests. You wouldn't have any warning, the team would just turn up randomly and pick two players, out of a hat, to test.

On this occasion they turned up at a training session. I was in the changing rooms when they arrived and greeted them before finding them somewhere to carry out their duties. I then went out to take the register while the boys were doing their warm-up.

'Listen up boys,' I said. 'The drug testing team is here, and they are going to need to test two of you.'

No sooner had I spoken, five players scarpered! I faced a real predicament and decided to seek Gareth's advice.

'You have to tell the CEO,' he said. 'We can't have this.'

Gareth was right, of course. With the help of the club doctor, we spoke to the five players involved and got to the bottom of the problem. Four of them thought they might be in trouble and panicked, but one owned up to steroid use – there was no way we could brush this under the carpet. I had to report him, which led to him being banned for two years. Initially I felt terrible as it wrecked a promising career, but the more I thought about it the more I realised he had let his teammates and the club down and had no one to blame but himself.

On another occasion I was tasked with getting new attire for the players – shirts and suits – as it was important that we all looked the part. Now I have no fashion sense – my wife had been dressing me for years – so, with hindsight, I made the mistake of asking the flamboyant Rupert Moon to help me out. We visited a men's outfitters and were shown all manner of styles, but he insisted on getting these green jackets – we looked like a bowls team!

I was also involved with the media from time to time, and that included being interviewed by Ray Gravell live on television during games. It was always quite stressful, not least because I would be concentrating on the game, but you could never turn Gravs down, he was such a likeable guy. I always insisted speaking in English however, despite it being on the Welsh-language channel S4C as, even though he would give me a quick heads-up of what he was going to ask beforehand, I never knew when he would go off-piste!

*

One of the most testing episodes took place when we were targeted by the Inland Revenue. I have already spoken about the amount of money that was sloshing around the supposedly amateur game in the '90s, so it was no surprise that it eventually came to the attention of the men in suits. Lots of money hadn't been declared and they wanted to recover it. They had set up a field office in Bristol, thinking that they would go into Wales and come back with millions of pounds.

Llanelli was chosen as one of their targets and I had a call from our Chief Executive telling me that they had been on the telephone and had asked to interview me and six of our players – talk about being thrown in at the deep end! It was no surprise that I had been singled out for interrogation as I was the go-between between the players and the club. I had a little office, about the size of a telephone box, in the weights room down at Stradey, with a sign on the door saying, 'The Buck Stops Here'. It was a strange situation to find myself in as I wasn't any good at maths in school.

I didn't really know what to expect, but when I arrived I realised that I recognised one of the inspectors. He was a guy called Stuart Slyman and I had played football against him when he was the centre forward for Ystradgynlais. When I said that I knew him, they asked if I wanted to put in a request to have him replaced, but I said it was fine. I took a seat and turned to Stuart and said, 'You never scored past me.'

'Yes, I did!' he replied and we started talking football, which relaxed the whole situation. Then they switched on and started firing questions at me. I wouldn't call it the Spanish Inquisition, but I must admit I was very nervous as I was handling a lot of money. Fortunately, I had a red book in which I would write down everything that I had handled and where it had gone. I had a list of all the players and their expenses, and I had to go through it all with an assigned tax expert.

Players were receiving bonuses, but it wasn't life-changing money. It was an open secret that all the clubs were breaking the amateur code big time. I can remember altering my own travel expenses once and our treasurer, Gwyn Walters, called me in and said, 'Anthony, can I have a word?'

'What's the matter?' I asked.

'Well, it's your expenses form. Are you still living in Ystradgynlais?'

'Yes.'

'Well, you used to put down 30 miles and now it's 45 miles.'

I said, 'I used to live in the front part of Ystradgynlais but now I live in the back.'

'An extra 15 miles? How big is Ystradgynlais?' he asked incredulously.

We all tried it on.

After grilling me, the inspectors directed questions at the players and they replied, 'I don't know. Anthony knows.'

They would see that a player had received some money and ask, 'What was that for?' I would turn to my book and reply, 'We told him to eat a certain diet and he has to wash his kit.'

'Can we see their receipts?'

'Nobody told me I had to keep receipts,' I replied. 'I have it written down here. I can show you what day it was spent and where it has gone.'

They even turned up at players' homes and knocked on the door, but the player would say, 'Anthony Buchanan deals with it all.' It was truly the case of the buck stops here.

In the end I was able to satisfy them, and although the club did end up having to pay tax, it was nowhere near what the Inland Revenue had expected to garnish. This was pretty much the case with its raid on rugby as a whole, but it did act as a warning and, in hindsight, added to the argument for the introduction of professional rugby.

*

One of the more uncomfortable episodes came when we played away against Ulster. Martyn Madden had been selected on the bench and was sat in the stand when he was racially abused by a couple of home supporters. I witnessed it myself and called a steward over and said, 'I want those two evicted from the ground.' The steward tried to brush me off and refused to intervene. I rarely lose my temper but I was seething. 'Now listen to me,' I told the steward, 'I'm going to walk on that field and stop the game if you don't remove those two racists from the ground.' He could see that I was dead serious and thankfully he called a colleague and the racists were shown the exit. There is no place in rugby, or life, for racism.

*

The game went open in 1995 following the World Cup in South Africa. I wouldn't use the term 'professional' because money was already in the game. Also, the term professional was questionable because the majority of players were still amateurs in outlook, but now they were being paid, and it took a long time for them to adjust.

The move was instigated by the WRU Chairman Vernon Pugh, who was also the then Chairman of the International Rugby Board. It was an interesting time to say the least.

I agreed with the move as the game had to change. The world was getting smaller. When I first went to Fiji and Tonga it took 35 hours, but now international travel had improved significantly and we were at a stage where southern and northern hemisphere teams needed to play one another far more regularly. We needed to have big gates, big crowds and big payments in order to grow the game.

The southern and northern hemisphere teams were also at loggerheads over who was doing what, and the term amateur had become a little bit farcical as it was obvious that some international teams were already pretty much professional. Remember, I had seen it for myself in New Zealand in 1987 and 1988. The All Blacks were training full-time, whereas we were still working during the day and training twice a week for a couple of hours. The reality of the game going open allowed us to play catch-up with the other countries with regards to fitness and the conditioning side of the game, but it wasn't going to happen overnight.

This was highlighted when Llanelli played New Zealand again in 1997 and we were hammered 3–81. The lesson was obvious, we had to become more professional. The All Blacks had put real daylight between us, and we needed to catch up. They were really on it that day, they were exceptional and really taught us a lesson. I remember Sean Fitzpatrick telling me after the game, 'You guys play rugby to get fit. We get fit to play rugby.'

Our players just couldn't match them physically. The coal mining industry, the ironworks, all the heavy industry was coming to an end, and the boys were now pushing paper around instead of shovels, yet the physicality of the game was growing. Our strength and conditioning coaches were trying to find ways of bringing us back to at least some sort of parity. We had to look at setting up academies and getting promising players, at the ages of 16 or 17, to learn how to lift weights and to prepare themselves physically.

We realised that young players were arriving nowhere near the physical standards required for professional rugby – the skills were there but we needed to develop them. I do believe that, run correctly, academies are a true asset to the regions. The problem, I believe, is players can be looked upon as being like a pizza – everybody wants a slice of them! They have lost the opportunity to play the game, to develop their playing skills. We don't always get it right, and we do miss some – a prime example being Josh Adams who lived near Parc y Scarlets but ended up having to go across the bridge – but the system does work and has produced some world-class players.

*

I had swapped my office from the tiny storage cupboard in the weights room for a proper office beneath the stand and started getting paid as team manager, but I maintained my day job, although it was a huge commitment between the two. I was constantly on the telephone and was doing 15-hour days. It came to a head around the time that Ieuan Evans had a compound fracture of his ankle playing against Cardiff. It was a dreadful injury. I remember he was lucky that the surgeon Dr Fairclough was at the game and he came on the field and reset his ankle there and then, which probably saved Ieuan's career.

After a long rehabilitation we picked him to play his first

game back against Glynneath in the Cup. I can remember going into work and the wife of one of the managing directors was not impressed at all because the phone line had been blocked constantly by media enquiries as to whether Ieuan was playing or not – his return had caused worldwide interest. I had a real telling-off because the business couldn't function! That led to the club providing me with my first mobile telephone. I realised then that the responsibility of team manager was growing and growing.

*

We soon discovered that paying wages did not necessarily bring success, and there was so much work to do. The players were still behaving like amateurs. We had to encourage them to identify the correct behavioural patterns in order to adjust. Graham Henry faced the same problem when he took over coaching Wales; players had to change their lifestyles to accommodate the professional game.

I really felt that it was going to take as at least four to five years to get anywhere near where we needed to be. It was down to people like Gareth Jenkins, fitness experts Peter Herbert and Richard Tong, and a team of strength and conditioning coaches coming in advocating how players should change – such as changing their drinking habits, quitting smoking if they smoked, and looking at what and when they were eating.

We switched to daytime training sessions and increased their frequency as we started putting systems in place. But we were handicapped as we didn't have the facilities at Stradey Park for it all. We also had to operate on a limited budget. We just did the best we could. We built a new weights' gym and were fortunate that we had two training pitches which we could use in most weathers.

Our backroom staff was growing all the time. The games

were being videoed and we employed analysts who were sat in the stand during games, giving immediate feedback to the coaches on things such as how many rucks had taken place and in which part of the field, how many scrums and lineouts there were and where they were, and how many penalties were being conceded. We were analysing the opposition ahead of games and players would analyse their own game and receive feedback from the coaches in terms of how they could develop. All this meant we had to look for more space.

The selection process, like everything else, altered as we became more professional, and the coaching team grew. When it came to selection, while I never had an actual vote, Gareth and Alan, to be fair to them, always asked me for my opinion and it was very rare that I disagreed with them. They always listened to what I had to say, especially around the front five.

It was a big adjustment for the players but their families struggled as well in many instances. Many a player's wife came to me to complain about the amount of dirty kit they now had to wash once training had gone full-time. I used to think to myself, 'Has he told you how much money he is earning?'

Players' wives caused me a number of headaches. They didn't want to be left behind any longer and we had to find room on match days to accommodate them and their children as well. I suppose we could have handled it all better, but it was all new to us. We were creating a new history within the organisation and we didn't have enough space.

Some players took to it like a duck to water, while others struggled to adjust because they couldn't deal with the time commitment. It wasn't a straightforward adjustment by any means. People may think that it would be wonderful being paid to do something you love, such as playing rugby, but it became a huge commitment and it didn't involve life-changing money. Players' contracts usually matched what they had previously earned, perhaps a little bit more, over three-year contracts.

*

The biggest implication of the game going open was finances. Whereas before, you would put in all that commitment and effort for the reward of a major overseas tour every few years. It totally changed the make-up of the game in terms of how it was run, both on and off the field.

It soon became obvious that in terms of club finances and the paying of players, we were headed towards a train crash. There just wasn't enough money in the game. There wasn't enough money coming through the gates and there wasn't enough money coming in from the Welsh Rugby Union.

Something had to change, and it did in 2004 when David Moffett, who was CEO of the WRU at the time, introduced regional rugby. The move, which saw the formation of five regional sides (which became four after a year when the ill-fated Celtic Warriors folded) at the top end of the game, was met by a huge amount of resistance as it tore up over 100 years of tradition.

The regional concept didn't go down particularly well and it's fair to say it has struggled ever since. But, in reality, we had no choice in the matter. You can reflect back on whether they were good or poor decisions, but they were decisions which had to be made. The clubs would have all gone bankrupt as we were all trading with little or no money coming in.

There was talk of us combining with our old foes, Swansea, but we made a very strong case for being a region, the Llanelli Scarlets, which I believe was right. But the Ospreys are the only true region. That said, we tried our best to engage north Wales, which was part of our regional vision. Gareth and I spent a lot of time going around the clubs up there, and we even played some 'home' games in Wrexham but, whatever way you cook it, it's still a four-hour return journey.

We were quite well supported when we played in Wrexham, and we still get supporters coming down from the north. It was a great experience to go up there and play some home games. Could we have done more? Possibly yes. Were we getting a huge return from it? No. We tried to develop rugby as a culture up there, but you must remember they are much closer to Manchester and Liverpool, and we were always competing against football.

I honestly still believe that we should embrace the whole of Wales as a rugby nation, and not just play the game along the M4 corridor. But I generally believe that north Wales as a region is a long-term project. It would require the right amount of financial support. Saying that, I do believe that Conwy Council did all that it could to develop rugby in the area, but it was an uphill task to deliver it to the level which was needed. At the end of the day, I don't think there was ever enough money to make a difference.

*

The old committee style had gone, and the Llanelli Scarlets now became a Chief Executive-led business. Our CEO was Stuart Gallacher. Stuart was like Marmite, people either liked him or they didn't. I found him a real character of a man. He had been a tough, uncompromising player in his day. After going to rugby league he became a dual code international. Although on my first encounter I didn't know what to make of him, we became very close, and I can't speak highly enough of Stuart.

Stuart oversaw a huge transition. As the game was becoming more professional, we realised that the game itself – the manner in which it was being played – needed to change. It needed to become more attractive, we needed to grow a bigger audience as bills had to be paid and that would come from television money, gate receipts and sponsorship, which all depended upon a marketable product.

None of the Welsh regions were getting big enough crowds. I still get asked this today, 'Why don't we get bigger crowds? Why don't we get more support?' People always point to Ireland and the huge support that Leinster enjoys but, if you look at it, Dublin must have a population approaching 1.5 million, so, relatively speaking, 16,000 people isn't a huge percentage of that. Ulster Rugby Club is situated in Belfast, again another large city. Munster has the whole south west of Ireland and enjoys fanatical support, but Connaught on the west coast has far smaller crowds, reflecting their local population which is very rural.

This may go down badly with some, but I don't think the Rhondda Valley fully supported the Celtic Warriors and so it was wound up. It was tragic, as Pontypridd and Bridgend are real hotbeds of rugby talent, but they just didn't get the gates.

In Wales we will always rely upon funding directors – without them we would all be gone. The game can't wash its own face; we still need moneymen to put their hands in their pockets, with very little chance of getting any return from it. I don't think Welsh rugby, and people in general, give enough credit to the moneymen such as Peter Thomas in Cardiff, Martyn Hazell at the Dragons and Mike Cuddy at the Ospreys. There are bound to be people who disagree with me, but we have to acknowledge the debt we owe to these people who came to the rescue of Welsh professional rugby.

In our case, there is no doubt that Huw Evans saved the Llanelli Scarlets with his generous support; without him we would have folded. He became a huge part of the region and words can't begin to describe his contribution to our survival. He supported us above and beyond financially. Without his support we would never have been able to come out of the black financial hole we had found ourselves in.

Things had become so desperate that, at one point, Stuart Gallacher phoned me up and said I had better come in. He sat me down and said, 'We're not going to be able to pay the wages. We're done.' Thankfully, the phone went at five to four in the afternoon with the message that the wages had gone through – thanks to Huw Evans. There was huge relief, but we knew then that we had a real problem with our debts running away from us.

With Stuart at the helm, we started from a very low base and had to achieve a position where we could finance ourselves. Sometimes we were living from hand-to-mouth. The pressure was immense, but Stuart bore it all and never shied away from making the difficult decisions; none more so than when we had to sell Stradey Park to the Welsh Rugby Union. It wasn't something we arrived at lightly, a great deal of soul-searching had gone into it. We reached the conclusion – if you have got an asset you have to utilise it. And we utilised it.

Our financial worries had taken a turn for the worse after we had been let down by a would-be investor. He was interested in bringing 'a substantial sum of money' into the club. I was part of the team which met with him, and soon after a firm came in to measure up for new training facilities which would enable us to bring ourselves up to a level to compete with the best.

There was a big push for overseas players, such as your Frano Boticas of this world. So with the promise of all this cash we went down the route of bringing players in – some were good signings, some were not so good. We ended up building a new stand more cheaply than what we had paid for Botica. Our 'benefactor' told us to tell him which players we wanted, and he would use agents to go out and approach them. Steve McDowall came over from New Zealand as a go-between and we went down that route while looking for players.

The problem was the money never materialised. It was like a fairy godmother situation where he promised to deliver everything we ever wanted but it never happened. I honestly believe the club did everything it could to verify the integrity of this investment. Unfortunately, we had stretched ourselves to a financial breaking point by the time we realised it.

Stuart faced a huge amount of resentment from some supporters over selling Stradey Park. It was a tough time for him, but he stuck to his guns. I can remember Huw and Stuart saying we would buy it back. And we did. I really feel he showed the leadership that delivered the stability and what we have today. He should be remembered as one of the greats who delivered a secure future for rugby in west Wales.

*

Our money worries were at the heart of perhaps the most contentious decision we made as a region – the move from Stradey Park.

Our supporters were horrified to learn that after regaining ownership of our spiritual home, we were talking about moving out. But, once again, we had no choice. Stradey Park was like an old Morris 1000 which had 150,000 miles on the clock. It was well loved and widely renowned throughout the world, having hosted all sorts of games and massive occasions, but it just didn't have the facilities for the professional era. The roof was leaking, the shuttering had gone, and it really needed a complete overhaul. We had tried our best to bring it up to date, including a new stand on the Tanner Bank to accommodate the Argentina v Western Samoa 1999 World Cup game. But, after the Hillsborough disaster and subsequent new regulations, there was a limit to crowd capacity on terraces, which badly hit our gate receipts.

We also lost a significant part of our income from car park charges once the crowds were cut. It had provided significant income. Not only did supporters have to buy tickets, but they also had to pay for parking. The joke was the players received income from an area of the car park depending on your pulling appeal. Myself and Laurance Delaney had an area that could barely accommodate a MINI!

I completely understand why so many people were against the move, but they were living in the past. We had to look to the future and the future demanded that we had the facilities to accommodate professional rugby. There was no one more emotional than me during the last game. I was most probably the last person to leave, as I locked the door behind us as we left.

My co-author, Geraint Thomas, wrote a moving piece about Stradey Park soon after its closure, which perfectly sums up the old ground's place in the hearts of Scarlets supporters.

Stradey Park 1879–2008

When the final whistle was blown for the last time there was, for once, no rush for the exits. The terraces and stands remained packed with subdued supporters, many fighting back tears, others stared across the pitch and down the years to their favourite moments, and all contemplated the end of an era.

After nearly 130 years of rugby at the famous old ground, the last tackle had been made, the last try scored, and the last excited roar of the crowd had drifted off over the town to fade into the sky.

Never did a sports ground so epitomise the heart and soul of a town. Quite simply Stradey was, and still is to many, Llanelli. Generations of children enjoyed a rite of passage, passing through its gates to stand in their fathers' coat-tails on the crowded terraces, to marvel at a mix of skill and sorcery that would ignite a lifelong Scarlet passion.

Even in the depths of winter, on drab Saturday afternoons or mist-murky midweek evenings, its four floodlit beacons guided the faithful in their thousands to Stradey. The town outside would be put on hold as the hushed, heart-in-the-mouth silences and screaming roars echoed down the deserted streets, shaking the windows to startle the left-behind cats and dogs, letting the whole world know that Llanelli were playing and that it should be there.

Max Boyce sang about being there following that never-to-be-forgotten day, 31 October 1972, when little Llanelli shocked the rugby-playing stratosphere by beating the mighty All Blacks, 9–3.

There were many other moments to be there... a first international scalp in 1908 when Australia were humbled 8–3; a narrow one-point near-miss against the brutal South African sides of 1912 and 1970; and 1992, when Ieuan Evans dived under the posts to seal a 13–9 win against the then World Champion Wallabies.

The list goes on. Just as one sublime sidestep or bone-shuddering tackle doesn't make a game, Stradey was built upon innumerable mesmerising moments. After seeing its first match, against Neath in 1879, it went on to become a breeding ground for legends who carried the name of Llanelli forward with Wales, the Barbarians and the British and Irish Lions.

And now, Stradey is not there – except in the hearts and minds of the faithful – having being replaced by Parc y Scarlets in 2008.

Time will move on but Stradey Park will never be forgotten – close your eyes and stand tall, place your hand on your Scarlet-blood-pumping heart, lift your head to the breeze and hear the roar of 15,000 people standing, as one, to salute their Scarlet heroes.

Amen

*

Once the decision had been made to sell Stradey Park – it was bought by a housing developer and today has streets named after famous Llanelli players – Stuart Gallacher played a huge role, alongside Huw Evans, in getting our new home built and the Scarlets into a position where we could hold our head above water and survive. Carmarthenshire County Council also played its part in providing a loan which attracted a lot of criticism from some quarters, but in my opinion the council should be applauded for helping preserve top-flight rugby in an area in which it meant so much to people. A brownfield site became available near Trostre Steelworks and it became Parc y Scarlets, one of the most impressive rugby stadiums in Europe.

The new stadium was opened in 2008, and it was like exchanging the keys of that Morris 1000 and taking delivery of a brand-new Ferrari. The only drawback was it had no character at that stage. The game had changed. We needed a 15,000-seat stadium. We were able to include a small terraced area, because some people will always prefer to stand with their beer to watch a game, but health and safety forbade large numbers.

It is a fantastic stadium despite all the detractors. It was supported by other people, but Stuart and Huw drove the idea through to fruition and deserve every plaudit possible. It was the dawn of the new professional game in the area.

CHAPTER 11

A Special Treble and the European Adventure

ONE THING THAT didn't change immediately was our love affair with the Schweppes Cup – it was still a major event in the early days of professionalism – and we continued to be the Cup kings of Wales. It is quite incredible really that I was involved in 17 Cup finals as a player and team manager, winning 11 and only losing on six occasions.

While we still threw everything at having our away day in Cardiff in May, with the advent of the structured Heineken League we obviously set our sights on winning that. Whereas the Cup was like a sprint, with a relatively few number of games, the league was a marathon with a different set of challenges thrown up around having to maintain a level of form and consistency throughout the season. We embraced the challenge and finished runners-up to Neath in the first campaign and went one better two years later and won it.

That 1992/93 season was a special year for the Llanelli Scarlets and our supporters as it saw all the hard work and forward planning, instigated by Gareth Jenkins, come to fruition in spectacular fashion with a unique treble. We beat Swansea 17-6 to lift the Schweppes Cup, we won the Heineken League, and we beat the 1992 touring Wallabies.

I had been fortunate enough to play against several touring international sides for Llanelli – and come out on top – so when Australia arrived in November 1992 I was in a privileged position to help prepare the side for what turned out to be another glorious chapter in the club's proud history.

It was a Saturday game, which meant we faced their Test team who were the reigning world champions and packed with world-class players. It also meant, being a Saturday, that more people were able to attend. It was another massive occasion down at Stradey and was like a mini-international. I still felt the nerves on the evening before the game, even though I was no longer a player, but there was nothing I could do on the field of play this time. Another difference I noticed was that you were always on duty as a team manager, and you were the first person a player called if there were any issues – as I was soon to find out.

There was a big dinner at the Stradey Park Hotel on the Friday evening as part of the build-up to the game, which for once I could attend as I was no longer a player. During the dinner I was summoned to reception to take a phone call from one of the players, who shall remain nameless to save him embarrassment.

He had called to say that he couldn't get time off work and wanted to know if the club would pay for someone to cover his shift. If not, he said, he wouldn't be able to play. I was gobsmacked, to be honest with you, that a player would leave such a request to the very last minute, the night before our biggest game of the season.

I just told him, 'Make your mind up. Do you want to play or not?' He told me he wanted to play but he needed to pay for cover at work. Eventually I told him that it wasn't something we would usually do but, as it was such an important game, it was certainly something we would consider, and to leave the matter with me.

I must have been taken aback by the player's request because when I returned to the table Gareth Jenkins saw my face and wanted to know what was the matter. When I told him he agreed that we should pay – it turned out to be worth every penny as he was one of 15 heroes who helped Llanelli to a famous 13–9 victory!

The high point of the game was a try by Ieuan Evans. The move saw Rupert Moon feed Colin Stephens from a scrum on their 22, Simon Davies came in on a decoy charge, and Ieuan Evans came off his blind side wing onto a pop pass and hurtled through the parting of gold jerseys to touch down under the posts! It was a fantastic try, right off the training field. The celebration, which saw Rupert jump up and bump chests with Ieuan believe it or not, had also been practised in training by the pair!

The win was sealed with a fantastic drop goal by Stephens near full-time.

At the final whistle, supporters invaded the pitch and carried players off on their shoulders, bringing back memories of the famous '72 victory against the All Blacks. To me, the '92 result should be on a par with that game – when they drank the pubs dry – which has quite rightly gone down in history, but in my opinion this was also a memorable result.

*

I even managed to get a game in myself that season after receiving a phone call from the former Wales flanker Paul Ringer, asking me if I fancied a day out playing for the British Transport Police. They had a game against their rivals, Thames Valley Services, up in Reading, and wanted a couple of ringers to strengthen their team. I had no idea what Paul's link with the police was – perhaps he had struck a deal with them to get off some misdemeanour!

I agreed and we travelled up by train. We were having a light meal before the game when I was introduced to a high-ranking police chief. The sergeant who was in charge introduced me, saying, 'This is Anthony Buchanan who has come up from Wales to help us out.'

He looked at me and said, 'I hope you haven't come here to cause mayhem and thuggery like last year.'

'Of course not,' I replied, 'I'm not that type of player.'

I later cornered Paul and the sergeant and asked, 'What was all that about?'

It turned out that it was a real grudge match, and the previous year's game had been marred by fights, with broken bones and someone having their ear ripped off!

'We've brought you in to strengthen our pack,' the sergeant said, 'and we've got a couple of boys up from Truro.' I looked over and saw two giant Fijians. They were massive men, both over six foot six.

'You've got the wrong guy if you think I'm going to start breaking heads,' I told him.

When I ran on to the field their tight-head was staring at me and giving me the evil eye. 'This is going to kick off,' I told myself.

I was named captain and before the first scrum I said, 'Right boys, let's give it everything we've got and see what they're made of.' I smashed into that tight-head and lifted him over the second rows, and he ended up sitting on top of his Number 8. The verbal abuse he gave me turned the air blue, so I did the same to him the next scrum, and the one after that. In the end I said, 'Listen! If you stop the nonsense, I will leave you be. But carry on with the abuse and it won't end well for you.' He was quiet after that.

I soon realised that the standard was pretty poor and on a par with second-team rugby. We won the game quite comfortably and my opposite number came up to me in the clubhouse after the game and asked, 'Who are you?'

'I'm nobody,' I replied, 'just a prop from Wales.'

His face lit up and he said, 'I've been to Wales a few times. I've got a mate who lives in Ystradgynlais.'

'Have you ever been to the rugby club there?' I asked.

'Yes, a couple of times,' he replied.

'Well, the next time you're there have a look on the walls, and you may find out who I am,' I said, knowing that a photograph of me with my Wales cap hangs there.

They had arranged an erotic dancer as the after game entertainment, and when the time came to catch the train home Paul managed to get her to drop us off at the station in her taxi. She was wearing this big coat with nothing underneath, and as she got out to wave us off she flashed us! I can remember thinking that if she had been arrested it would have been quite a task for her to explain to the Transport Police where she had just come from!

To thank me for helping them out, the Transport Police told me I could travel first class by train anywhere in the country. This soon came in handy as our unique club treble became a quadruple when we were named World Team of the Year and 15 of us were invited up to London to receive the trophy – I was able to get us all free first-class rail tickets!

Ieuan Evans had been named World Player of the Year. David Campese was the Overseas Player of the Year and, as he was by then a professional player, he received a set of golf clubs. Ieuan, still being an amateur, was given a box of golf balls!

Now Ieuan was due to link up with the Lions ahead of their tour to New Zealand. So he gave me his trophy and golf balls to take home for safe keeping. After the function we headed into London for a few drinks, and as we were leaving to catch the train home our flanker, Gary Jones, said to me, 'Where's Ieuan's trophy?' I had left it on a bar! Fortunately, it was still there when I hurried back, and I was spared the embarrassment of having to explain to Ieuan that I had lost it.

*

The introduction of the Heineken Cup in 1995 was another huge transformation. The competition saw the top sides from Wales, Scotland, Ireland, England, Italy and France compete against one another for the right to be crowned the best team in Europe. There had been a tremendous amount of excitement around the introduction of European rugby, and it was seen as rugby's equivalent to Champions' League football – an elite competition designed to bridge the gap between regional and international rugby.

It led to some amazing European nights down at Stradey Park, and it feels as though I can remember each minute of every one of them. Our supporters really got behind us and games were sold out. The atmosphere was unbelievable and the standard of play so much higher than what we had previously experienced. That said, the Heineken Cup was a massive step up for us and a huge learning curve – not least when it came to playing away.

One of our first travel experiences was a trip to the south of France to play Pau. Having arrived the day before, we visited the ground as part of our preparations. Frano Botica, who was our outside-half and goal kicker, favoured sand over a kicking tee, so I informed one of their ground staff that we needed to have some at our disposal. I was informed that it would be taken care of but, come kick-off the next day, there was only one small bucket of sand available. As the game wore on, and Frano took more shots at goal, the sand began to run out. Eventually, our kit man looked up at me in the stand and said, 'There's no more sand.' We had only taken four penalties; it was 15 minutes into the game. I hurried down to look for their groundsman, but he was nowhere to be seen. Suddenly, every Frenchman I saw couldn't speak a word of English. Then I remembered seeing a building site down the road as we had arrived. So I grabbed a black bag and ran out of the stadium, climbed a fence in my suit, filled the bag with sand, and ran back. As I made my way back down the tunnel, we were awarded a penalty and Frano was calling for sand!

We lost the game, but the trip had been a wonderful experience, so different to what we had been used to. Pau was a beautiful place, in the shadow of the Pyrenees, and the hospitality after the game was fantastic. Mind you, the hospitality got a bit too much at times when they started supplying the boys with as much absinthe as they could drink – the stuff is hazardous! It was like rocket fuel and our boys were all over the place. I was like a sheepdog running everywhere trying to get them back on to the bus.

*

On another occasion we were playing against Stade Français in Paris, so we went over on the Eurostar. It was another huge learning curve as their president was a multi-millionaire telecommunications mogul, and had bought in players from all over the world. We got hammered by 50 points. It was an embarrassingly heavy defeat, and I was accosted by some journalists after the game demanding my reaction. I turned to them and declared, 'We will win the return fixture at Stradey.'

'You have got to be joking. You were totally outclassed,' came the reply.

'I'm telling you now, we will win. The boys aren't used to the travelling. We're still in our infancy of learning how to play abroad. It has to come through experience, but we will beat them at Stradey.'

As all true Scarlets supporters will tell you – I was correct!

*

Adjusting to the task of playing away in Europe was a challenge to us all. As team manager I had the added burden of having to organise many of the logistics and to make sure everyone was looked after and happy – that included the backroom staff as well as the players.

My ability was tested when we played Bourgoin in January 2000. When it came to food the players had their own routine and ate set meals prescribed by the strength and conditioning coaches, so I decided to take the coaches and medical team out for a meal the evening before the game.

Stuart Gallacher, as usual, was holding court in the restaurant when the waiter came over to take our order. I decided to ask the waiter what he recommended. 'Calf's liver,' he replied.

'That sounds nice, I'll go with that.'

Now Stuart, who was always good company, looked at the menu and ordered the seafood platter. Once the waiter had left, Stuart turned to me and said, 'How could you ask the waiter what to order?'

'Well,' I replied, 'I think he would have a better idea what was good than me.'

Then it came to the wine, and while everyone else ordered a red I ordered a white wine.

Stuart turned to me again and said, 'You Valley boys are uneducated. You're not having this; you're not having that. You haven't got a clue.'

I said, 'You just order what you want and let me order what I want.' It was all in jest.

We had a lovely evening and retired to bed excited about the challenge that lay ahead.

I was woken the next morning by my phone. It was Stuart.

'Get me a doctor,' he murmured. He sounded terrible and I was really startled. I got our doctor, went to reception to get a key and we rushed to his room.

The first thing that hit me was the smell – it wasn't pleasant! There he was, laying on his bed, wrapped in a towel – he was unbelievably ill.

Ieuan Harris, our doctor, examined him and said, 'You've got food poisoning.' He was given some advice and confined to bed rest whilst we went to the game. As we were leaving the room, I held his hand and said, 'Don't worry Stu, us Valley boys have everything under control!' The air behind me turned blue as we left his room!

Anyone with a superstitious bent may have seen Stuart's sickness as an omen, as the boys were really on edge before the game. You could sense the nervousness in the changing room. Scott Quinnell was throwing up in the toilets and complaining that he wasn't well enough to play. Dafydd James was another wracked with nerves.

'Bloody hell,' I thought, 'we're falling apart here.'

Gareth did his best to lift the mood and got the boys out on the field. They kicked off, Scott Quinnell caught the ball, ran the length of the field, swatting tacklers aside, and scored under the post. Seven points up. Five minutes later Dafydd James rounded everyone down the wing and touched down under the posts. Fourteen points up. At half-time the score was 6–22 to us, and all the while I was getting phone calls from a sick Stuart wanting updates.

'How are we doing?' he asked.

'We're up by seven.'

'How are we doing?'

'We're up by 14.'

It was unbelievable, all one-way until, shortly after the start of the second half, Stuart asked, 'How are we doing?'

'They have just scored,' I said.

The reverse flow of scores continued until I reported, 'They've scored again. It's 28–32.'

'I'm not calling you again,' he grumbled, and slammed the phone down.

It was an incredible game. Martyn Madden, who was on the bench, was doing moonwalks down the touchline during the first half – when we were racing away with it – and in the second half we were all on the edge of our seats, biting our fingernails! Thankfully, we held out and went on to win 30–36. It was a huge result – our first victory in France. I think we were the first Welsh side to win out there.

I've already mentioned the French hospitality – they really did pull out all the stops. They would invite the town mayor and all the local dignitaries; it was always a real event. On this occasion they had over a thousand people packed into a big marquee, erected especially for the occasion.

When we arrived I was approached by one of their committee who asked, 'Where is your president?'

'He's ill in bed,' I replied.

'Then you must sit with our president,' he said.

'No, no,' I said, 'I'm just the team manager.'

'You must,' he insisted, 'it is the protocol.'

I reluctantly agreed, having little choice and not wanting to offend our hosts. There was a knock on a table and the announcer boomed out, 'We would like to welcome the Llanelli Scarlets, and their president... Anthony Buchanan!' With that, everyone got to their feet and clapped me to the top table. You can imagine the ribbing I had from the boys later.

I took my seat and shook hands with those around me and then the waiter appeared and poured a small drop of red wine into my glass. I noticed that everyone had stopped talking and were now looking at me expectantly. As guest of honour, I was expected to approve the vintage. I picked up my glass, took a sip and nodded my approval without really knowing if it was nectar from heaven or dishwater! Everyone applauded and the red wine started flowing.

Now I'm not a fan of red wine, so I turned to the interpreter and asked, 'Is there any chance of me having a beer?' He looked at me in horror.

'I could get you a beer,' he eventually said, 'but first let me tell you that the gentleman on your left is our president and the most important wine producer in all of France. That drink in front of you now is the most expensive red wine in all of France. Do you really want to insult your host?' He'd made a fair point.

We obviously tried to return the favour when they came to Stradey. Our caterer was Clive Hopkins, who owned Blanco's Restaurant in Port Talbot and the Towers Hotel in Skewen. It was top-drawer food and always presented well. I will never forget that on one occasion the waiters brought in the turkeys on platters and the French thought that they were chickens and were pointing to each other and making clucking noises! It was so funny watching the waiters trying to explain that they were turkeys.

When it came to hospitality, to be honest, in the early days down at Stradey we struggled a bit with space. We tried to get marquees in, but they were sell-out games and space was always in short supply. People would come from all over Wales to watch our home games – even in France we would get people travelling from places such as Pontypridd or Newport and coming up to us after games to say hello.

*

It was my job to get the team to the various destinations around Europe, which didn't always go as planned. The players called me Tony's International Tours – abbreviated to TITs – with the catchline, 'We'll get you there but can't promise to get you home!'

One example was when we had played against Leinster in Dublin. We arrived at the airport to fly home and I looked up at the departure board to see our flight had been delayed. I went to the information desk and asked what was going on, only to be told that our flight had then been cancelled.

'What do you mean, cancelled?' I asked.

'We've had a problem with the plane.'

'When are you going to get us out of here?' I asked.

'I don't know,' came the reply.

I had 30 players and backroom staff sat there waiting to go home. I called Gareth over and said, 'We've got a problem, the flight's been cancelled.'

'They can't cancel the flight,' he said.

'They just have.'

'What are we going to do?'

'I will have to make some phone calls,' I replied.

I was told that we could get on a 7pm flight; it was now 8 in the morning. There were some earlier seats on flights to Bristol and so everyone started getting on different planes. I took the remaining players back to the hotel to wait. Then myself, Gareth, Stuart and Gareth Williams, another of our medical staff, decided to go out for a meal, and we had a good drink.

Travel was always unpredictable, and we were always in a panic as the club faced quite a hefty fine if we didn't arrive in time for games. On another occasion, which highlights this, we were due to play Roma out in Italy and were on the coach to Heathrow when my mobile phone went. It was Nick Webb, the BBC commentator. He said, 'Do you know Alitalia have gone on strike? There are no flights out until tomorrow morning.'

We were playing the next day, so it was panic stations. I spoke to Stuart; he spoke to Huw Evans and Huw rang his solicitor, who started making phone calls. It was decided that they would try to get us on another flight from the East Midlands.

When we arrived at Heathrow I got everyone in a holding area and went down to the Alitalia desk at the terminal. It was obvious that the girl behind the counter was having a very bad day. As I walked towards her, I could see that she was a typical Italian, very highly strung and there was a lot of gesturing going on. When we were face to face, I said, 'Llanelli Scarlets. We have a European game, we must be on a flight.'

She looked me in the eyes and said, 'No!'

'Yes,' I replied.

'No!' she repeated.

'I want to see the manager,' I said.

I looked to her right and could see this woman, who equally looked as though she was having an awful day, approaching with steam coming out of her ears. She looked at me and said, 'No!'

I said, 'Yes. We're transferring over to East Midlands.'

Again she said, 'No.'

Gareth, who had accompanied me to the desk, said, 'I think you've lost this argument. Just ask them for some food vouchers so we can feed the boys.'

I said, 'No, I'm not giving in.'

I got back on the phone to Stuart.

'What's happening?' he asked.

'They won't transfer our flights,' I told him.

'They have to,' he replied.

'I know, but they won't.'

Stuart said, 'I'll phone you back.' He got back on the phone to Huw Evans who called his solicitor again. I don't know who they spoke to but the phone on the desk went shortly afterwards and the look on the manager's face, when she picked it up, was priceless – she had been ordered to transfer our flights.

The only problem was they could only take 24 of us and our party was 32. I had to make a quick decision as to who to leave behind to catch a later flight. It was tight, and as I sat down in my seat they closed the door for take-off.

When we arrived at Roma's ground the next day their president came up to me and said, 'You are all invited to our 75th anniversary dinner this evening.'

We were taken to this fantastic venue; it really was one of the most impressive buildings I've ever seen. After the meal their president got up and thanked us for joining them and I thanked them for inviting us. Then their president got up again and said, 'Can all the Roma wives stand, and can all the Llanelli players stand, and can you dance together?'

'This is going to be one bad idea,' I thought to myself.

To be fair to the ladies, they came over and led the boys to the dance floor – I don't think many of our players would have won *Strictly*! Then their president came over, placed a rose between his teeth and invited Stuart, who had arrived on a later flight, to dance with him. I have seen some sights in my time, but I can honestly say the pair of them dancing was the funniest thing I've ever seen in my life.

After the dancing we were treated to some singing from our hosts, but then they wanted us to return the favour. There must have been around 500 guests in the room and none of our boys would get up to sing.

Their president said, 'This is very disappointing.'

In the end Stuart persuaded me to get up and give them a song. Reluctantly, I climbed to the stage, where there was a band waiting, and sang the old fail-safe, 'Delilah'.

It was a great occasion.

Afterwards, the boys started to cadge lifts back to the hotel with the Italians. Gareth grabbed my arm and said, 'Come on Bucks, it's chaos out there. Let's have a drink in the bar and catch them up later on.' While we were in the bar their second row, an American by the name of Luke Gross, who eventually signed for the Scarlets, came into the bar.

'Are you guys OK?' he asked. 'If you need a lift, you're welcome to jump in our car. There are only three of us.'

'Great.' We followed him into the car park, and he had a Fiat Punto. Now he was six foot seven and more or less sitting on the back seat to drive. How we fitted five rugby men inside I do not know. I can remember going around the Colosseum, and only managing to catch a glimpse of the magnificent sight out of the corner of my eye as we were all piled on top of one another!

*

Eventually we decided to go down the route of chartering our own aeroplane. Our first charter saw us share a flight to France with Caerphilly, who had come up through the divisions. We dropped them off on the way to the south of France and picked them up on the way back – it was new territory for all of us.

Another time we were playing Glasgow, and as the game was in Perth, at St Johnstone's ground, we decided to charter again. We had travelled to Cardiff Airport and were all sat there waiting to be called when the pilot, with a high visibility jacket on, strolled in and asked for me.

'What's up?' I asked.

'It's the plane,' he said, 'it's overweight.'

'What can we do about it?' I asked. This was all new to me.

One option was to only fill the fuel halfway and stop in Liverpool to refuel, but that would mean that the airport at the other end would have closed by the time we got there.

'We can't risk that,' I said.

'Well then,' he replied, 'you will have to reduce the weight on board.'

'My people carrier is in the car park outside,' I suggested. 'We can drive the kit up in that.'

'That may work,' he said.

Fortunately, Nigel Davies, who was our backs coach, offered to drive because he was never an enthusiastic flier, and he was accompanied by Wayne James, our kit man.

This was in the days before heightened security, so I drove out onto the runway and parked next to the plane, opened the tailgate, laid the seats flat and we stuffed as many kit bags as we could inside. There was barely enough room for Nigel and Wayne to get in and they set off immediately for Perth.

At first, I didn't envy them that long drive, but when I took a closer look at our plane I wasn't so sure. It was a propeller-driven rust bucket, with seats like deckchairs which rattled and shook non-stop once in the air. I was sat next to a window and it was so slow I'm sure I spotted Nigel overtaking us near Manchester!

We eventually arrived and were quite surprised to discover the airport was nothing more than a single runway with a tin shed serving as the terminal. We transferred by coach to our hotel and were met soon after by Nigel who had made the journey in around six hours – they must have taken lessons from Lewis Hamilton on refuelling to get there so quickly. I dreaded speeding tickets coming through the post for weeks afterwards.

As for the game, we were ahead right up until the final three minutes when Glasgow took the lead for the first time and held on. It was a miserable night all round as it was freezing – for once I was happy to be retired. It was around –10°c and there was snow everywhere but fortunately the field had undersoil heating.

The players were so disappointed they asked whether they could go home early. I gave the pilot a call and he said, 'It's your plane, you can go whenever you want.' We quickly made our way to the airfield, eager to get home, but when we entered the shed the pilot came in and said once more, 'We've got a problem.'

'What is it this time?' I asked.

'The plane has frozen,' he replied.

'What can you do about that?'

'We need to link it up to the de-icer. Have you any strong boys?'

We all had to go out onto the runway and push the plane to the hangar so they could de-ice it. That was my first experience pushing a plane! We were told to give it an hour and we should be OK to take off.

We returned to wait in this freezing cold shed and, without seeing our situation in the same light as the Busby Babes, you could not help but think that we were taking a massive risk. We came really close to taking the boys back to the hotel to wait for better weather the next day.

Obviously, we eventually managed to take off safely, but that flight was no pleasure trip and I wished I were sat next to Nigel in my car a number of times I can tell you. I wasn't too fussed on chartering a plane after that.

*

Getting used to the travelling, the different food and strange beds, it all had an effect on the players. The quality of the food at the beginning was very poor, especially during the first year or so. I had a falling out with Peter Herbert, our conditioning coach, once after Leigh Davies, who was the captain, came to see me saying they couldn't eat the food and the boys were starving. I sorted the situation out by taking them all to McDonald's. When Peter found out he wasn't happy at all. I had to explain to him that the pasta the hotel had provided tasted like cardboard and that having a McDonald's was better than not having any food at all.

*

Fortunately, as we grew into the role of playing in Europe, the food and accommodation got better. People wanted us to stay at their hotels as it was good business for them, and they would go out of their way to accommodate our needs. We would say, 'If you want us to stay with you this is what we want.' We would lay out our eating requirements and so on. They really did bring it up to standard in the end.

This no doubt helped us develop into a successful side which could hold its own with the best in Europe, although we never did quite manage to achieve our ambition of winning the Heineken Cup. We gave it a damned good shot however and reached the semi-final twice while I was team manager, but both times ended in last-minute heartache that still hurts today.

On the first occasion, in 2000, we faced Northampton at the Madejski Stadium in Reading which was supposed to be a neutral venue. But when we arrived at the ground all we could see was a sea of scarlet. The support we had was phenomenal. I think every man, woman and child in Llanelli had made their way up the M4 to support us that day. It was an unbelievable occasion, even for a semi-final, and something we hadn't experienced before.

There was nothing to separate the two teams, and with the scores level after 80 minutes the game went into extra time. Unfortunately, the history books will tell you that we fell to a 31–28 defeat with the last kick of the game. Paul Grayson landed a penalty after Ian Boobyer had infringed in a ruck on the halfway line. We were devastated; we had come so close and we were good enough to have won.

Two years later we reached the semi-finals once more and faced the English Cup kings, Leicester, at the City Ground, Nottingham.

I had a phone call a couple of days before the game from the organisers saying that they wanted myself, Gareth, and Scott Quinnell to attend a press conference in Nottingham on Thursday afternoon.

'Are you serious?' I asked. 'It's going to take us four hours to drive up there, for an hour's press, and then another four hours coming home. We're not going to do it.'

'It's written into the agreement. You are contracted to attend press conferences and will receive a heavy fine if you don't attend,' was the reply.

I said, 'You can do what you like. We're not coming,' before adding, 'The only way you're getting us up there is if you send a helicopter.'

'I will ring you back,' he said.

He called back ten minutes later and said, 'Right, we've got a helicopter to pick you up.'

On the Thursday morning we climbed into the helicopter which had touched down in Stradey and off we went. The pilot was an Australian and was typically laid-back. He was quite chatty and told us that he regularly flew the TV presenter Gabby Logan around the country. I was surprised to see that he was following the motorways to navigate, and when we approached Birmingham he pointed out some chimney stacks and said, 'When we get there, we turn left.'

We arrived in Nottingham and he touched down on the halfway line of Nottingham Forrest's ground. We climbed out, made our way inside for the press conference, came back out and got into the helicopter again, all within 90 minutes.

We took off and the pilot said, 'Sorry guys, I have to land for fuel.'

'Where the hell do you fill up a helicopter?' I thought to myself. We went to East Midlands Airport where he filled up and paid with his credit card.

He took a different route on the way back. We crossed the Malvern Hills, and the Brecon Beacons came into view. It was fantastic. Gareth and I were sat in the back and Scott was up front with the pilot. I had been given a camcorder by the BBC to shoot some footage and the pilot turned to me and said, 'Turn that camera off and we will have a bit of fun.'

I complied and the pilot took us on a ride the like of which I had never experienced in my life. He nosedived down towards the Carmarthen Fans and skimmed the surface of the lake, Llyn y Fan Fawr, with the nose seemingly a couple of feet off the water. If you don't know the area, the lake is at the foot of a mountain which rises up like a green wall, and the pilot banked the helicopter on its side as we skirted the mountain.

All I could hear was Scott screaming in the front and Gareth and I were hanging on for dear life. There was a rambler on the mountain top who dived to the floor as we came flying over the top! I doubt that the biggest rollercoasters in the world would have come anywhere near to what we had just experienced.

We then picked up the M4 and made our way back to Stradey. I couldn't believe how far rugby had come: from local rivalries to Europe-wide, high-stake competitions in such a relatively short space of time.

As for the game itself, it was a case of history repeating itself in a manner that Scarlets supporters still struggle to come to terms with today. Again, we were in front and headed into injury time, only for a last-minute penalty to snatch a first appearance in the final away from us.

Martyn Madden was accused of collapsing a scrum on the halfway line. I think it was really harsh to give a penalty. I'm obviously going to say it was not a penalty. If you are going to do it in the last minute of the game, and it's going to decide the outcome, that's a huge call for the referee to make. No one wants to give a penalty away, no one intends to give a penalty away.

What made it more agonising was the fact that once again it was a long-range penalty, in their own half in fact, and we had to endure the anguish of hoping it failed only to see it bounce off the crossbar, hit the post and creep over. It gave way to one of the most amazing sights I've seen in a rugby game – usually rugby crowds are mixed but, on this occasion, the two sets of supporters were segregated. When that ball finally went over, half the stadium was on its feet cheering and the other sank down in stunned silence, unable to believe what they had just seen.

That 13–12 loss was even more devastating than the Northampton result.

Years later I ran into the referee that day, David McHugh, and I said to him, 'That was never a penalty.'

And he told me, 'If I thought he was going to kick it, I wouldn't have given the penalty.' And I believed him. When you reflect back to that day, I honestly believe that the referee didn't want his decision to decide the game.

We had to try and lift the players big time following that defeat – I have never experienced such disappointment in any rugby game before or since. We had deserved to win. Leicester were the renowned Cup kings, yet we had matched them and done enough to win the game... and we were winning it until the last few seconds.

CHAPTER 12

Giving Something Back

MY TIME AS team manager ended soon after Gareth Jenkins and Nigel Davies had been appointed to the Wales jobs, but the region had offered me a new three-year contract which I initially signed, as they were looking for some consistency with Phil Davies and his new team of coaches coming in.

I had a lot of respect and regards for Phil. He had been a great captain of Llanelli and had cut his coaching teeth with Leeds Carnegie. You couldn't fault his commitment to the Scarlets. We discussed my role several times but, eventually, I felt it was time for Phil to place his own stamp on the region. After talking to Alana, I decided to stand down. I had served my time in the professional game and had no aspirations of stepping up again. I had no wish to jump on a plane and spend the night in a hotel before waiting for an 80-minute game which would make my weekend or not. I had given 25 years to Llanelli and there needed to be a clean sweep.

In all, I did ten years as a player and 15 years in the role of team manager. I believe I was the first team manager, certainly in Welsh rugby, and when other sides followed suit, Derwyn Jones, who took up a similar position at Cardiff, called me the granddaddy of team managers!

Out of respect, I called Gareth on the way down to hand in my letter of resignation and he tried to talk me out of it. Despite being with Wales, he always had the Scarlets' best interests at heart, but my mind was made up. I had just set up my own business alongside a former Quasar colleague, Anthea Davies, and I realised I could no longer commit myself full-time to my rugby role. I was constantly on the road with the team – it was obvious that the team manager position had become a full-time occupation. I was fed up with leaving the house at 7 o'clock in the morning and returning at 9 o'clock at night. My two daughters, Amy and Adele, were growing up and it was tough not being around.

Giving up the business wasn't an option. I had great customers who I was reluctant to lose. They had become my friends, and I also had a very good, solid income from the business. I couldn't continue doing two jobs. Yes, I was benefiting financially but it was taking its toll on me and I couldn't keep it up much longer.

I don't regret my decision as I'm proud of what I achieved in the world of business. We started off with a small office on an industrial estate in Skewen, and within a year or so I was back in Milland Road Industrial Estate, Neath, where it had all started with just me and Anthea. Later we employed Janine and Chris. By the end we were up to 28 people and had a successful business – Acorn Chemical Services – that we had built from scratch.

*

It was a strange sensation waking up on a Saturday morning and not having anywhere to be. I felt a kind of release, but when Alana asked me, 'What are you going to do today?' I replied, 'I'm going to watch a game of rugby.'

'I thought you had finished with rugby?'

'No,' I said, 'I've finished my responsibility with rugby.' The team manager's role carried a tremendous amount of pressure and I felt a weight lifted off my shoulders.

I went to watch Llanelli play in the Premier Division up in Llandovery, and I had a lovely day out in west Wales.

Not long after that the BBC invited me to do some work as a pundit for radio but, as they say, I don't think I had the face for radio. I did a couple of games, but it wasn't something I felt comfortable with. It just didn't work for me.

I was considering what to do next when there was a knock on my door from Ystradgynlais Rugby Club asking me whether I would consider taking up a coaching role with the club. I gave it some thought; the club was still close to my heart and I felt as though I wanted to give something back. So I decided to go down and meet the committee at their Monday night meeting.

I sat down and was told that they were delighted that I was considering coaching the club. Then the chairman addressed the elephant in the room, 'How much money do you want for coaching us?'

'I don't want any money,' I told him, 'but I have three stipulations which are non-negotiable.' There was something of a stunned silence before the chairman asked, 'What are they?'

'I want an ice machine for the changing rooms, a bus laid on for every away game, and the ability to change the food that players receive after games.' I had asked myself, 'what can I bring here that will make a difference? What hasn't anyone done before to engender team spirit? But without spending too much money?'

Looking around, I could see a few committee members with their mouths open. Then the chairman asked, 'Are you sure you don't want any money?'

'No,' I said, 'this is my chance to give something back. I'm not saying that I will do it for a long time, but I will certainly help.'

*

I needed a backs coach and was grateful that Stephen Bayliss – who had started off in Ystradgynlais before enjoying a successful spell in rugby league with St Helens which led to him winning a Welsh rugby league cap – agreed to come on board. I'm sure that if he'd stayed in rugby union he would have become another local boy to go on to play for Wales because he was an exceptionally talented winger. Andy Davies, a stalwart of the club, made up the trio of coaches. We also had Dan our first-aider and Gareth our physio, and Matthew Rees spent time at Ystradgynlais (he is now heading the Scarlets medical team) – it was a good backroom team. Off the field the club had built new changing rooms and I felt really optimistic that I could help take them forwards.

As I left the meeting the club steward, John Owen, who was a former hooker and quite a character, called me over. Now he had overheard our discussions and he said, 'If the club is buying a new ice machine, I want it for behind the bar. You can have the old one.'

I replied, 'As long as I get an ice machine in the changing rooms, I don't care.'

You may wonder why I was so intent on having ice on tap as it were. My experiences with Llanelli had shown me the value of putting ice on any injury immediately. It reduced the damage and speeded up recovery. I didn't want players missing training and spending longer on the sidelines because they weren't getting the proper treatment. I also wanted to get the message across that they had to look after themselves in order to be successful. I wanted them to automatically think, 'I've got a bit of a pulled muscle; I need to put ice on it.' The ice was there, I had bags and shrink wrap on hand, there was immediate treatment available. I told Gareth to monitor their injuries and let me know how severe they were – it all helped to change their mindsets.

The following Thursday the new ice machine arrived, and John called me over and said, 'Your new ice machine is here.'

'I thought I was going to take the old one,' I said.

'You have no chance. I'm keeping it.'

When I went into the committee room I understood immediately why he had changed his mind – it was tiny! If we were only having gin and tonics we would struggle to get enough ice! If I were a cynical man, I would say the committee had tried to get one over me, but I kept my thoughts to myself and took the new machine across to the changing rooms. We had a home game on the Saturday, so I filled it with water and switched it on.

The game came around and we had a good win. Immediately afterwards I told the boys, 'If there's anyone with any bumps or bruises, there's ice and shrink wrap here. I want you to treat that injury immediately.' I then went to the ice machine and, when I lifted the lid, to my amazement, it was full. In the club a bit later I was just about to tell John that he'd missed a trick by not accepting the new ice machine, because there was loads of ice, when he said to me, 'Did you get the extra ice I sent over for you?' It wasn't the new machine that had produced all that ice, someone had topped it up! I found that amusing.

When it came to the after-match meal I changed the traditional sausage and chips to tuna and jacket potato. When the players saw their meals they were taken aback. Their tight-head prop looked at his and said, 'What's this?'

One of our boys replied, 'It's a jacket potato.'

'Where's the sausage and chips?'

'Buchanan has stopped them.'

'Who the hell does he think he is?!' he shouted.

I thought I had better make myself scarce so I went into the bar.

This was my first game in charge – Division 5 West. We won the game; everyone was happy with the result – if not the food – and they all wanted to buy me a pint and tell me where we needed to improve. Although my first game couldn't have been further away from professional rugby, I really enjoyed the atmosphere and all the banter.

On the issue of diet, I didn't intend to try to get them to eat like professional athletes. But there were small changes they could adopt which would make a difference. It was all part of changing the way they thought, of making them act and think like winners. It did lead to, in hindsight, a very funny episode.

We had a big game against our rivals Abercrave at home in the Cup on the Saturday. My final instructions on the Thursday were for the players to think about their diet and to load up on pasta ahead of the game. On my way home I drove through the town and passed the local kebab shop, Yummies, and happened to glance through the window. Looking back at me from the queue was our scrum-half. I knew that he had seen me so I stopped, reversed back, looked at him and just shook my head. He looked mortified.

By the time I got home I had received a text message from his mother, telling me that he hadn't gone to Yummies for himself but to get food for his brother. I quickly sent a text back telling them not to worry about it but, unbeknown to me, the predictive text was on and it sent a load of nonsense.

On the Saturday I was at the club before the game when his parents came hurriedly up to me and said, 'Can we have a word, Anthony?'

'Of course, what's the matter Bev?'

'Your text message.'

'What text message?' I had forgotten all about it.

'The one you wrote after you saw Daniel in Yummies. We couldn't read it. Did it say he's out of the team for Saturday? He was getting that kebab for his brother. We haven't slept.'

Although it was a funny story it showed how the players and their families had taken the message of change on board.

*

The reason for demanding a bus for away games was down to building team spirit and cohesion. I had discovered that players had fallen into the routine of going to away games in cars. I wanted to get them into the mindset that we arrived as a team, played as a team and left as a team. After the game you pay your respects to your opponents and spend an hour or so in their clubhouse, socialising and forging friendships, before having a few beers and a sing-song on the coach home.

It was a bit of a challenge and I would constantly be asked, 'Are you sure you want a bus? Have you got enough players to fill it?'

'Look, this is what we agreed, and we will work at it,' I replied.

On one occasion, early on, I had a call from the club secretary, Alan Jenkins, and he said, 'Alltwen away on Saturday.'

'Yes,' I said.

'How are we going down?' It was only a few miles down the road and I knew what he was trying to say, 'Do we really need to hire a bus?'

I said, 'We could go down by train, but they pulled the tracks up years ago, and we can't fly down because there's no airport in Alltwen. So, I think we will go down by bus.'

He was quiet for a minute and then said, 'What size bus do you want?'

'Listen,' I said, 'I don't care what your argument is. We're having a 45-seater coach and we're all going on it to Alltwen on Saturday, and we're all coming home after the game on it on Saturday.'

*

I had lots of ideas on how to improve performance, but soon discovered that I had to temper my expectations as I was in a far different rugby environment from the one I had left. For example, I took a flip chart along with me to my very first training session and got everyone to gather around in the changing rooms and said, 'I'm going to write your names down and then you are going to do a three-kilometre run. As you come back, I'm going to write your times against your names. I will bring the times along next week and you can do the same run, and see if you can beat your times.' I thought it was a sensible way of easing them into improving their fitness. However, I sent them off and half the boys never came back! It was pretty obvious some of them couldn't even run three kilometres.

The process of coaching in that kind of environment – we were in the lowest league possible – was all about engaging the players. I realised there and then that if I introduced hard training sessions I was going to lose them. It called for a change of tack. Luckily, a friend of mine from my playing days with Ystradgynlais, Lyn Thomas, who had played a few games with Llanelli before tragically breaking his back in a mining accident, was playing wheelchair tennis in the area.

I asked him, 'Have you got any tennis balls?'

'I've got loads of them,' he said.

'Can you bring them down to training along with some tennis rackets?'

I introduced a drill where a ball was hit into the air and players had to run and try to catch it. There was lots of laughing, with balls bouncing off heads and shoulders, but they were running all over the place. But, most importantly, they enjoyed the activity.

I tried to make training fun but also effective, as I knew that if the side could raise its fitness by 15 to 20 per cent more than that of the other teams in the division, we would be successful. I started to realise that I had to get inside their heads, not to the extent you see at a professional level of course, but I had to get them to change their mindset towards the way they approached playing rugby.

In terms of the squad, they had started to rebuild the year

before. Remember, the club had made mistakes thinking they were going to take the Heineken League by storm, which nearly bankrupted them. Thankfully, they had since decided not to make payments to any player whatsoever, but this resulted in all the players who had come for the money leaving. On the other hand, the genuine local players, who had been peeved off with the buying-in of players, had all left, so we had to start over from scratch.

I realised this but there were still a few players around, and then a few more came back. Dai Love, who had played first-class rugby with Aberavon, returned, and I could see that we had the basis of a fairly decent team.

I still had contacts with Kooga and, after a call to Manchester, the players had new T-shirts and kit bags. I insisted the boys wear a polo shirt with the club's badge on the front after games, and we all warmed up in club T-shirts. I had no aspirations other than trying to improve them as a team. I just wanted them to know that something was different at the club.

*

Our second game was away to Gowerton. Gareth Jenkins called me in the morning and asked, 'Where are you playing today?'

'Down in Gowerton,' I told him.

'Oh, I'll come and watch,' he said. A little while later Nigel Davies called and asked the same question. He was living in Gowerton at the time and said he would come along to lend his support.

We had finished our warm-up and I was leaning against the barrier around the pitch when Gareth and Nigel turned up and started making their way towards me. They caused a bit of a stir, and when a few elderly Gowerton supporters who were sat behind me noticed that the Wales coaches were at the game, one of them said, 'Look, the national coach is here.'

'I wonder which players they're looking at?' replied another. I think they realised fairly quickly, once the game had started, that they were only there to give me some support. It really meant a lot to me. It was great to see that, even though I had left the Scarlets and was down at the other end of the rugby pyramid, I was still in their thoughts. Gareth actually came to a few of our games after that and would offer technical advice. He was really supportive. That's the measure of the man.

*

I knew the Ystradgynlais players didn't have the skills or fitness to play the Llanelli way, but I still wanted to encourage them to play good rugby. They responded as the season took off and we played really well. Our only hiccup came when we were drawn away in the Schweppes Cup to Cardigan. It was a fair old trek to the west coast, but I knew a guy who was a big Scarlets supporter who ran a pub just outside Cardigan, near Cenarth Falls. I called him up and said, 'Look, I'm coaching Ystradgynlais now and we're playing Cardigan in the Cup. Is there any chance you can put food on for us before the game if we call in?'

'Consider it done,' he said.

On the Saturday I got all the players on the bus and made sure they all had bottles of water. I said, 'Listen boys, it's a long journey. Let's make sure we're hydrated and prepare properly.' Then we stopped for food. It was all the correct type, and the players couldn't believe the way they were being treated.

Unfortunately, when it came to the game itself it was a disaster. We lost by 30 points.

In the changing rooms afterwards, I settled the players and said, 'Guys, that performance wasn't acceptable. I don't mind losing but we lost in a manner that let ourselves down.'

When we boarded the bus for the long journey home I could see that the players were genuinely disappointed. So I got up and said, 'Look, what we'll do is stop somewhere on the way back and we'll all have a pint together. We're all in this together, win or lose. We stick together. We may be out of the Welsh Cup, but we still have the league and the West Wales Cup to play for.'

We arrived at a pub just outside Carmarthen and, while I was talking to a couple of the committee, all the players piled off and went inside. Then, as I was about to go inside I heard this woman screaming. I rushed in and asked, 'What's happened?'

Someone, who was amongst the first to enter the pub, had noticed a buffet had been set up for an 18th birthday party, and he'd taken great delight in telling the players that I had put this buffet on as a surprise for them! Of course, the players believed him because I had laid on food on the way to the game. They descended on the buffet and filled their plates, but when the mother of the birthday girl entered the room she went ballistic.

'This is Anthony Buchanan's buffet,' someone insisted. I saw the funny side, but it was very upsetting for the family involved, for which I apologised profusely.

*

While I was delighted to be able to give something back, I also took a tremendous amount of pleasure in helping the team grow and develop into a useful outfit. Despite the Cardigan hiccup, we went through the league undefeated, only losing out on the title by one bonus point, and secured promotion. It was a really successful season with the icing on the cake being an appearance against Cefneithin in the 2008 West Wales Plate Cup final, which was held at Stradey Park.

I was able to secure the home changing rooms and I did my

best to make it special. I placed pictures of the players above the pegs and hung their jerseys up to greet them. I wanted the players to remember the occasion for the rest of their lives. I even brought Gareth Jenkins in to deliver the team talk – if there's one thing he excels in, it's motivating a team. He went through the history of the changing rooms, telling them of all the great players who had walked out from there to make rugby history – the players thought it exceptional. He wanted them to understand that they had to grasp the moment they were being given, and take their opportunity. They went out and won 52–10! We absolutely wiped the floor with them – and they were the team which had pipped us in the league by a point. Dai Love was man of the match. We played some amazing rugby and the pride I felt equalled anything I felt winning the Schweppes Cup with Llanelli.

*

Following that final game of the season Gareth Jenkins called me up and said, 'Look, as much as you enjoyed helping your local side out, would you consider coming back to Llanelli?' He had returned to the Scarlets in an advisory role, following his departure from the Wales job. I went down for a meeting with Gareth and Stuart Gallacher to hear them out. They had major concerns over the way the Llanelli Premier Division side was being run, not least the amount of money some players were on, and asked would I consider overseeing the running of the side as Head of Rugby?

I accepted on the grounds that I would not be on planes or in hotels. At that time, it was a Saturday game and midweek training. I was fortunate that Anthea, who was a Llanelli girl, understood my commitment.

I had enjoyed my season with Ystradgynlais immensely – it was the most humbling experience coming off the back of professional rugby and going into Division 5 West. It gave me a big insight into the community game. I realised how difficult it was, but it was rewarding. Any guilt I may have felt about my departure was softened by the knowledge that I was leaving them in a good place. A few seasons later Vernon Cooper, another Ystradgynlais boy who had graced Llanelli and Wales, followed in my footsteps by taking over. He took the side even further with a few promotions and a SWALEC Bowl Cup final victory at the Principality Stadium.

*

Although a new region had been created – the Llanelli Scarlets, which later became the Scarlets – Llanelli RFC, as with all the former Merit Table clubs, still existed and played in the Welsh Premier Division. Sadly, there had been a real fall from grace, and we had found ourselves at the bottom of the pile, flirting with relegation. My task was to turn things around. Most of what was needed was already in place but there was a lot to put right.

I fully believed in my task ahead. The WRU is a union of clubs, that's our strength, and the Premiership in the right hands is the tool which can service our regional game. We must keep the names of the history that we belong to, the likes of Llanelli, Swansea, Neath, Ebbw Vale, Aberavon, Cardiff, Newport and Bridgend. All these clubs, put in the right perspective and funded correctly, can deliver the next generation of players for the professional game.

Sadly, the Premier Division isn't well supported. Going away from the 3 o'clock kick-off on a Saturday was a huge mistake and the Premier Division doesn't receive enough publicity. We're in a different world today from the time I played rugby. We've got live television dictating when we play; we're challenged in 101 different ways, but we shouldn't allow that to distract us away from using the Premier Division as a tool for developing a clear pathway into the professional game. It has a huge part to play.

Unfortunately, in comparative terms, the clubs have to operate on a shoestring. The WRU doesn't provide enough money – it is so misguided – and it's up to the clubs to provide the answers. I hate to think where the rugby people are any more. Yes, we all have self-interest at heart as clubs, but it is up to the union to lead, to understand how it should be run – it doesn't know whether to have a s***, shave or shampoo. It's so mixed up; decisions are made that are poorly thought through. They are made by people who are not rugby people with the best interests of the game at heart.

*

With the lack of funding, my first task was to reduce players' salaries. We had to cut our cloth to meet our means, and the budget was part of my responsibility. This led to a number of difficult conversations. There was a lot of money being paid out to a lot of average players. When I looked into it there were some players earning more than some of the Scarlets players. We immediately offered them half of what they were on, which went down like a lead balloon. It saw players leaving, which was fine. We had to come into the real world.

This led to us having to rethink our player recruitment structure. We have overseas coaches dominating the regions. To be fair to them, they are here to make the regions successful, but they are not here to develop players. We realised that we had to develop our own players from scratch and were fortunate that we acquired a group of players who were good enough to make it in the professional game. We had the backbone of a team, with a front row including the Hopkins' boys Shaun and Aled, Craig 'Ripper' Hawkins backed up with Adam Powell, Nathan White and the likes of Dwayne Eager and Johnny Lewis in the centre. Most of these boys went on to play for the Scarlets.

We also put a structure in place where we looked for west Wales talent who were good enough to play at a higher level. Kevin Williams, who had been a Llanelli coach, came in and was very adept at going out and spotting talent. He found a group of players who went on to serve us outstandingly well. He also looked for players who had perhaps been overlooked by the regions, such as Kyle Evans and Josh Lewis, who went on to play for the Scarlets. That was our major aim, to develop players for the region.

Not everyone was happy. For instance, Bonymaen was an excellent club for producing promising players and giving them the opportunity to progress. I had a conversation with their former Wales star, Richard Webster, who accused me of taking Swansea players, but I told him I only took players who had been overlooked or not given an opportunity to play. That really was the key element. If they had the opportunity to play for Swansea, Neath or Aberavon, then fine, but if they were not given an opportunity then it was only right, if we felt they had the potential, to give them an opportunity with us.

Our policy proved to be very successful with a number of notable finds. We brought in a young Number 8 by the name of Ben Morgan who had been overlooked by the Blues. As soon as I saw him I thought, 'This boy is talented.' He went on to play for the Scarlets before moving to Gloucester and playing for England.

Then we had the Shingler boys, Aaron and Steven. The pair hadn't been picked up by any academy and had been playing cricket instead. We gave them a chance and they both went on to play professional rugby, with Aaron playing for Wales. The same happened to Owen Williams, yet another Ystradgynlais boy, who had been dropped by the Ospreys.

The biggest discovery was Liam Williams. I really enjoyed

watching him develop into the world-class player he became. He was another who had been overlooked by the academies – they don't always get it right – and he was playing for Waunarlwydd. His coach Rhodri got in touch and told me they had a young fullback who didn't look like a rugby player but was a tough hombre. I said, 'Send him down and we will have a look at him.'

There was something about him, and I wasn't quite sure what but I decided to offer him a contract. I met with Liam and his father at the Swansea West service station and produced a contract with a figure of £2,000. His father read it and asked, 'Is this £2,000 a month?'

'No, it's £2,000 a year,' I replied.

I could see that they were both disappointed but I said, 'This is not a contract to play professional rugby, it's an opportunity.'

Liam signed it and immediately made a huge impact. The rest is history. I was very fortunate to be there when Liam was presented with his first cap and his fiftieth cap and I felt immense pride.

His mother always says to me, 'Liam owes you so much.'

To which I always reply, 'Liam owes me nothing. We only gave him an opportunity. What he did with that is all down to him.'

*

There is also Jake Ball, who had come over from Australia hoping to make a name for himself. He had played for us up in Bedwas and I wasn't impressed and wouldn't pick him after that. Simon Easterby, who had taken over as Scarlets coach at the time, called me in and said, 'Look, this boy has come over from Australia looking for an opportunity. He realises he didn't have a good game on Saturday.'

'Good,' I interrupted, 'he was poor. For his own benefit,

if he can't bring a level of performance to our level, he's not going to bring it to a higher level.'

After that Jake knocked on my door and apologised for his performance and asked me to give him another chance. I told him, 'I'm not here to stop you having a chance at regional rugby, but I'm telling you, your performance last Saturday won't get you that chance.'

In all fairness to Jake, he took that on board and really knuckled down and has 50 caps to his name today.

*

We also wanted to offer young coaches the opportunity to develop their skills ready for stepping-up in the game. We gave opportunities to the likes of Ioan Cunningham and Dai Flanagan who went on to coach the Scarlets. Kevin George was also a part of the coaching team and was academy manager at the Scarlets and responsible for producing a number of international players. The same with physios and other backroom staff. It was a wonderful time of development for us.

The key to it all was giving these youngsters game time. The game at regional level had developed so much, but with all the different coaches and backroom staff wanting a hand in a player's development I realised the biggest mistake we were making was over-coaching. The coaches were becoming far more important than the players. They were dictating playing times, down to how many minutes they were getting on the field each week. We lost our perspective around what youngsters wanted to do. As it was, they were spending all their time on strength and conditioning – you can become a gym monkey, but you have to play to develop.

Our Achilles' heel is that these young players don't play enough rugby to learn the game. The more rugby you play, the more you understand the game. You can then work on your strengths and weaknesses. Liam Williams is a prime example of someone who played every Saturday, and once he developed his skills people recognised what he had to offer and he was given the opportunity on a bigger stage.

I'm proud to say that I helped build a highly successful side through drawing on players from our academy, late developers, and those who were targeted by the Scarlets. It was a tough environment, but we had huge success to start with. We went over to play Munster A, and beat them. Then went on to win the Welsh Cup and the league. The only problem was we became victims of our own success, as the Scarlets took a fair few of the boys to play for the region. When you look at that team there were seven players who went on to play for Wales – Rhys Priestland, Jonathan Davies, Aaron Shingler, Aled Davies, Liam Williams, Owen Williams and Gareth Davies – and Ben Morgan for England.

Once those players were elevated up, it left us very compromised. One week we would be at full strength and the next we were severely weakened, but that meant that we had done our job, and it was time to rebuild once more.

CHAPTER 13

Joining the Blazer Brigade

MY RUGBY JOURNEY experienced another fork in the road in 2014 when it was suggested that I put my name forward to take up a position on the Welsh Rugby Union board. Elections were coming up and, having spent seven or eight years attending Premier Division meetings, people like Byron Mugford and Meirion Howells, from Swansea of all places, approached me and urged me to consider standing for the role of National Representative.

The WRU's CEO, funding director, legal department and rugby side are paid positions but it's the board that holds them all to account – even the national coach has to come in and present to the board – so the board is both an important and necessary cog in the running of our national game. It wasn't something that I had ever considered to be honest with you. I had never sat on a traditional committee as we had broken the mould in Llanelli by setting up a small group of people to run the rugby side of the club. But, after a bit of deliberation, I decided to throw my name into the hat – Swansea RFC proposed me and Ystradgynlais RFC seconded my nomination.

There were two vacancies on the board after Gerald Davies decided to stand down. I was up against my former Llanelli teammate David Pickering, who was the sitting WRU chairman; former Wales outside-half and Dragons Chief

Executive Gareth Davies; Dai Davies (Newtown RFC) and Dennis Jones (Cefneithin RFC).

Despite my lack of experience I felt that I had something to offer but honestly believed that I had no chance of winning the vote. However, I did write what turned out to be a compelling letter of support, which set out to address a major rift between the regions and the union. I also outlined my experiences, not only in the professional game but also from my time with Ystradgynlais in the community game, as the second-class clubs had come to be known. I pointed out that the WRU wasn't really supportive of the regions, in my opinion, and failed to provide the funding required to grow and develop the success we all wanted.

A few weeks later I was sat outside my home, having just come back from walking the dog, when my phone went. I answered to find Martin Rees of the WRU on the line. He said, 'Congratulations, you've just been appointed one of our national representatives. Keep your head down because it's just been announced to the global media.'

I sat there and reflected on what I had just been told. One, I didn't think that it was newsworthy worldwide, and two, something major must have happened and that could only be that David Pickering had lost his seat on the board after 11 years. My reasoning was correct. In fairness to David, he was very gracious in defeat considering all that he had lost.

The position didn't just represent a district of clubs. I had been elected to speak for all the clubs in Wales. My appointment meant I had to stand down from my role with Llanelli but I consoled myself with the fact that I was leaving them in a far better position than the one I had inherited.

My surprise rise through the administrative side of the game took another unexpected turn when I attended my first WRU board meeting and was voted in as one of the WRU's representatives on World Rugby (formerly known as the International Rugby Board and the governing body of the sport globally). I had gone from someone who refused to play the game at school, and didn't play his first game of rugby until the age of 22, to being responsible for the development of the game worldwide! It was a dramatic turn of events.

My new role as a WRU representative was unpaid. While a small number of people are paid to run the game at the top end, rugby relies upon thousands of people giving up their time purely for the love of the game. I didn't expect any financial reward but I did receive expenses of course.

It was another adventure in rugby that I never imagined I would experience. Some would term it a gravy train but I resent that accusation – I was still running my own business while facing constant meetings. I would always print out any board papers and read them through thoroughly before meetings to be up to speed. Then I'd have to drive to Cardiff, or fly out to another country – it all took up time.

I remember saying to Janine at the Acorn Chemical Services office, 'I need a holiday,' and she chuckled to herself.

'Why are you laughing?' I asked.

'Well,' she replied, 'you've already had a fair bit of time away.'

'How much?' I asked.

She looked at the office diary and said, 'Well, since November you've had 31 days off.' I had missed a month of work in a four-month period, only I wasn't sunning myself on a beach, I was attending WRU or World Rugby meetings. It also required a lot of commitment involving numerous trips abroad, which may seem glamorous but travelling can get monotonous at times. I'm not complaining, I was fully aware of the time and commitment element before I put my name forward, but I want people to understand that it isn't one big jolly. These people should be recognised for all that they do to safeguard the game we all love. I take my hat off to all those who have put their name forward.

You attended major international home and away games,

which I always found very informative as you had time to sit down with representatives from other unions and hear how they were progressing and dealing with the various issues that are presented to the game. We discussed all aspects of rugby, not least how the shift to professionalism had challenged all involved.

One thing I will say, in all of my global travels, people were very complimentary about Wales. They would always remark how could such a small country be as competitive as we were.

Of the other home unions, Ireland had a pretty strong board with a lot of former players. Scotland were very similar to Wales, whereas England were very strong, a big wealthy organisation with a lot of clubs. The difference in England is the RFU don't fund their clubs, they fund themselves.

All the unions are non-profit organisations, with any profits being ploughed back into the game.

Before being elected I used to go to every Wales home game with Alana, and I would meet up with my friends in the former players' bar, the WREX room, and have a few beers. I missed that by going onto the board, and although I met some wonderful, really interesting people during the dinners on international days, at times I used to long to be with all those outside in the bars and clubs.

*

World Rugby runs the game worldwide. It holds two seminars in London each year, and discussions on all aspects of the game take place. Bill Beaumont was elected as Chairman of World Rugby in 2016, replacing Bernard Lapasset.

During my first meeting I was invited to sit on the Rugby Committee, which was chaired by John Jeffrey, the former Scotland and Lions flanker. Joining us from the northern hemisphere was the former French player, Bernard Laporte;

then there were two representatives from the southern hemisphere, Mark Robinson from New Zealand and Brett Robinson from Australia. The Argentinian, Gus Pichot, was Bill Beaumont's Vice Chairman of World Rugby.

The task for the Rugby Committee was to look at all the on the field of play issues. Our first meeting was held in Fiji – where I had enjoyed my first overseas tour with Wales, and I probably spent more time in the air travelling there and back than I did on the ground.

I found the meetings very informative, with senior players often invited along to share their thoughts on any changes we were considering. I always found that although you sat down with such iconic players, they were very much down-to-earth people.

On one occasion Richie McCaw came along to address us and it was a real privilege to meet such a legendary All Black. He was such an immense player; he played the game close to the edge and put his body on the line, and when he said something you listened. There was one instance, however, where I made the suggestion that there should be an end to the Number 8 keeping the ball in the scrum and calling for a double shove. It would result in a penalty and the ball would be kicked down the touchline, a lineout and a drive for a try. I wanted to encourage them to get the ball out, so I called for the penalty to be reduced to a free kick. It resulted in a bit of a discussion and, let's just say, I didn't win!

*

One of the major issues we addressed during my time on the committee was the scrum. We felt that it was an area of the game which needed urgent attention – it had become a mess at international and club level. It seemed as though every scrum would inevitably collapse and require a reset. Referees had to make the often difficult decision as to who was responsible for the failure of the scrum completing. It left them with an impossible task and they may as well have tossed coin to decide who to penalise.

Each scrum reset took between one and two minutes. When you have 10 to 15 scrums in a game that can sometimes lead to 20 minutes or more of players being on the floor with the ball not in play. Crowds were beginning to get fed up with it. We had to come up with a way to keep the scrum stable but still competitive.

I like to think that I made a contribution as a former front row player. My recollection of finding my way as a prop, and having to learn how to survive in the scrum, gave me a great insight into what front row players faced.

The problem was, some teams were using the scrum as a dominating factor. While it's lovely for the purists, we had to consider the people buying tickets to watch the game and we had to make sure the scrum, whilst being competitive, returned to being a mechanism to restart the game.

I thought that the key to it all was most probably a coaching issue, where it had evolved into selecting three big and massively powerful men instructed to drive over the ball rather than hook it back. This had taken away the skill of the hooker. The opposition had adopted the same strategy and you often ended up with stalemate, with the ball stuck in the middle of the scrum, not going forward or back, and eventually going up or collapsing. Unless the scrum-half fed the ball into the second row, the scrum was never completed.

One thing I had learnt from my playing days was an understanding of how the ball should travel from the Number 9 to the Number 2 to the Number 8. The ball had to be struck and the timing between the 9 and 2 was crucial to the ball travelling to the back end of the scrum in one movement. The 8 could then make a decision whether to keep the ball in or release it for 9 to play the ball away. Our decision was that the hooker had to strike the ball with his foot. The combination of 9, 2 and 8 had to come back into play. It had to be competitive and rugby had to remain for everybody – players of all sizes.

We brought in a framework – with the help of international hookers and props – around how the scrum was set, and stipulated that the hooker had to strike the ball. If the scrum-half put the ball in without the hooker striking it, it would be a penalty. The scrum-half had to put it in to the hookers – if it went into the second row then they were penalised. I don't think the television cameras show it clearly, and often the commentators who complain it wasn't straight are wrong.

I'm sure there are lots of people who have a view on this but I can assure you that the referee has been instructed to penalise anyone who doesn't. In my time the ball was put in down the middle and the hooker had to reach and strike the ball – returning to this was out of the question.

Nowadays you have big, powerful men and, from a safety perspective, you cannot allow someone to stretch his leg out in such an environment. Remember, these guys are now exceptionally strong athletes, and both packs generate huge amounts of power. We had to be extremely careful – one broken spine would be one too many. Improving player safety is always the highest priority. The design was to have as competitive a scrum as can be in the presence of such power. It was a huge challenge to come up with a solution.

We also had to defuse the charge – where the two front rows ran into one another on engagement. We ruled that the two packs had to start from a closer position – this was more or less already in place but not always enforced.

It was all about helping the referee make the right decision over who was collapsing the scrum. Everyone claims it isn't their fault. It's not easy refereeing a scrum but there are fundamental things to look out for – leg positioning, the bind, arms and shoulders. To look at where a prop positions his feet or whether he follows forward or not, if they are hinging, pretending to take the weight and then stepping back – there is a lot going on that the referee has to consider.

Although our solution improved the situation, it still presents a challenge. The referees still have to make difficult decisions, but when you consider the vast majority of them have never been in a scrum as a player, it is more clear-cut. It has worked to a degree – the scrum completion levels improved up to 65 to 70 per cent. You have to remember that any law changes have to apply to all levels of rugby. Any decision made at the top has to apply in Ystradgynlais, Trebanos and Tenby as well. It filters down to the refereeing managers in each union and then down to their districts.

It was rewarding to see the changes being implemented and the scrum remaining competitive.

*

Once we had drawn up a new set of orders, referees and coaches were made aware of the changes, and they were tried and tested in live games. It was an extremely interesting journey in rugby terms. I thought I knew the game, having been involved for such a long period of time, but I certainly had never viewed it from a refereeing perspective. It was a real eye-opener.

*

It wasn't just scrums. We had to look at all aspects of the game – lineouts, restarts, rucks, mauls and the tackle area.

World Rugby were implementing changes in order to try to make the game safer. We had huge discussions around the overall safety of the game, not least the proliferation of head injuries.

The safety of players has to be paramount in every referee's decision – and we realised that this burden of care couldn't sit entirely on the referee's shoulders. Refereeing had to become a team of four, with your referee assistant one and two, plus a television match official (TMO). It has taken a while but people are now on board with the whole concept. Players now realise they have to be conscious of the laws, not only with regard to foul play but reckless play, where players may not intend to carry out foul play but they throw themselves into a situation where they come into contact with the opposition and cause them harm. This is especially relevant in terms of reducing the number of head injuries, and such instances now warrant a straight red card. If you make contact with someone's head, intentionally or not, you run the risk of a red card.

I had to endure several conversations accusing us of making the game soft. I think today people will recognise that we did what we had to do and player welfare has improved, but in the early stages many saw us as trying to take the macho element out of rugby.

I believe what we did was correct – you only have to look at the great concern around concussion today. There had to be a rethink from everyone, from the coaches and players to medical protocols, referees and laws of the game. The safety of players had to be sacrosanct.

If players refused to change their habits then we had to introduce sanctions, which today have led to a proliferation of yellow and red cards. Hopefully the volume will drop off as players realise that, unless they follow the laws, they can very much disadvantage their side. Coaches have to play their part as well and make their players aware of their responsibilities.

As I have said previously, if some of the games I played in were refereed under today's standards, half the team would be sent off. It goes to show how far we have come in making the game less violent and safer.

*

Another part of my duties was to attend referee camps. We would bring the top referees in and have a discussion around the latest issues before providing a framework of what was going to be asked of them on an international stage, remembering it had to filter down to the community game as well.

It was a real eye-opener for me. I had to change the way I had watched the game for more than 30 years and see it from a referee's perspective.

We have to invest in young referees and make it absolutely clear that the referee is the sole arbitrator of the laws, whether he or she is at the Principality Stadium or Penlan playing fields in Swansea. They have to have the respect of all. They won't always make a decision that everyone agrees with, but there can be no disputing that decision.

Referees sometimes end up making a decision which determines the outcome of the game – remember our two last-minute Heineken Cup semi-final defeats. And that carries a huge responsibility for them to get it right.

The introduction of TMOs has helped, and the system is improving as we go along, but we can all reflect on numerous games where a debate was held in the bar afterwards whether or not the referee had made the correct decision.

Whenever I went out and watched a game with my friends over some beers, and they would all be questioning a decision made by the referee, I would say, 'If we didn't have referees we wouldn't have a game.'

For the very future of the game, people need to remember that referees will make mistakes but we all must accept that they are in charge and not overly protest. The media has its part to play as well.

Players have a responsibility to respect the referee as well and not end up like football players. To be fair, on the whole it is not a problem in rugby. It has always been like that. In my time we would never backchat the likes of Clive Norling or Derek Bevan. You had respect for the referee, whether you agreed with them or not. The problem is players are only human, their adrenalin is pumping and they sometimes think a wrong decision has been made – sometimes it is – but I honestly believe that 80 per cent of the time referees are correct and the other 20 per cent of the time there are different interpretations of the decision.

On the other side of the coin, I think the integrity of our referees is outstanding. You used to come across 'homers' who would always favour the home side – that's why we found it so hard to win away in France – but I genuinely believe that referees today are far more professional and clued in. A lot of money has been invested in their training, and their career pathway is clear.

We have some great young referees coming through the system, who you can see cutting their teeth on the seven-a-side circuit, and their fitness standards are huge and you can see their quality and commitment.

*

I was to receive one further honour at this time – that of being appointed Chairman of the committee for world refereeing appointments. This included working closely with Alain Rolland, World Rugby's Referee Manager. Also on that committee was Nick Mallet, the former South African coach, Joël Jutge of European Rugby, Lyndon Bray from SANZAAR, and Mark Egan from World Rugby, who was the referees' high performance director. The role also included the World Rugby Sevens Series, working with Paddy O'Brien and Craig Joubert, as well as the women's game. As noted, I was Chairman of the committee for the selection of referees for major tournaments or tours. It meant a lot more international travel, often on my own, which took a lot of commitment, but I had told myself that if I was going to do the job, I wanted to do it to the best of my ability.

I was surrounded by people who had been referees all their lives, but I like to think that I brought a coach and a player's point of view to the table.

Before any major tournament we would bring in the coaches and their captains and go through the protocols and what was expected of them so that they were well aware of how games were going to be refereed. I sat down with people like Warren Gatland, Joe Schmidt and Eddie Jones. Referees would then spend time with coaches and identify various issues, such as a tendency to creep off-side in previous games.

Our choices didn't always win widespread approval and there is no doubt that, due to the intensity of the game and the influence a referee has on the outcome, there were some referees who were not favoured by various countries. They even went as far as saying they didn't want certain referees, as they couldn't guarantee their safety from the perspective of the crowd in the stadium. I never tolerated any of that.

The selection process was quite simple. You had your top-level referees. But, as you do with players, you also had to consider the next generation and give them an opportunity to gain experience at the highest level. The number of international games was growing, and we realised we needed to increase the pool of talent.

When selecting a referee for a game, firstly you had to look at neutrality. For example, on Lions tours you couldn't select any of the home nations' referees. The referees were usually French or Australian, South African or Kiwi, depending on where the tour was held.

There was an elite pool of around six referees who would get the top games. You also had to allocate assistant referee one and two, and the TMOs. You would look at which referee had refereed particularly well and needed to go on to the next level to gain more experience in a highly intense Test match.

We would attend refereeing camps and analyse their performances and go through their decision-making. It was a real education for me being given a sheet of paper for the first time with all the different decisions, from free kicks to penalty and yellow and red cards, and being shown different situations and having to make on-the-spot decisions. We had to develop consistency in refereeing. If a referee made a decision in one game, another needed to make the same in the next. But, of course, all referees are different in personality and their approach. A lot of work was carried out by Alain Rolland with refereeing managers from the various rugby unions to get consistency.

Alain is seen as a bit of a controversial figure, especially in Wales as he is the one who gave Sam Warburton that red card which more than likely cost Wales a place in the 2011 World Cup final. He was correct to send him off. He had carried out a tip tackle and Alain followed the letter of the law.

Alain was hard-working and committed to the task. He travelled the world and spent time with referees, and he worked his socks off. He may not have been everyone's favourite person but I always found him very honest and direct. I had regard for him.

*

I was involved in two World Cups – England in 2015, in which I had more of a watching brief being newly appointed, and Japan in 2019, in which I had a far more hands-on role when it came to the referees.

We held a two-week team building camp with the referees in Japan before the tournament started. It was an opportunity to put in place frameworks on how they would apply the laws of the game – consistency is key – and build team spirit. It was a great experience and I can honestly say that you got to know people.

One of the team building challenges was to climb a mountain to a sacred waterfall. We were met by a guru who instructed us to stand beneath the water and chant in order to clear your thoughts. That was one experience I will never forget! You had to approach the waterfall barefooted, and the stones were quite sharp, but as all the referees had to do it I thought I had better join in.

I really appreciated the fact that they welcomed me in and, I hope, they respected my views. I know there will be some of my former front row colleagues calling for me to hang my head in shame for selling out to the enemy!

I was fortunate to meet many fine referees, but to me one stood out above the rest – Nigel Owens. Nigel is hugely regarded by everyone, wherever he goes. I had the honour of presenting him with a silver salver out in Fiji to mark his 75th international match.

I believed that Nigel Owens was the best referee in Japan. People have asked me why he didn't get the final. He had done the 2015 final, and I have to agree with them that he deserved the honour again, but it fell to Jérôme Garcès. Jérôme had been a top referee for a long time and was due to retire – whether sentiment came into his selection I cannot say, but he did a great job.

*

The World Cup in Japan was a tremendous experience and I genuinely believe the game developed as a result; it brought in more fans worldwide, not least in Japan itself. From a personal point of view I feel Wales missed a golden opportunity of reaching our first final, but the boys gave it their all.

However, one of the downsides for me was the Rob Howley affair. For those who have been living on the moon, he was caught breaking the rules when it came to placing bets on rugby matches, and was dismissed from his role with the Wales team.

I was in my hotel room when the news broke and received

an email from World Rugby which said I had to go downstairs and immediately do a course on ethics and what was expected of me. I think they realised that I hadn't completed the protocol. I wasn't the only one.

I don't want to comment on the rights or wrongs of Rob's actions but I think it was tragic, as I had hoped that he would become our next high performance coach in the WRU when he decided that his coaching days were over. But, rules are rules. I still think he could be one day, and believe he would be an asset. He carries a lot of experience.

*

My term on the WRU board ended in 2019 and I had to decide whether I wanted to renew my commitment for another three years, if elected by the clubs once more. But, I had a more pressing matter to take care of closer to home, so I decided against it.

Not to be too dramatic, the very future of Llanelli RFC was under threat, as I saw it. The club had returned to hovering around the bottom end of the Premier Division and I felt it would be a great shame if the club found itself going out of existence. I felt that the timing was right for me to go back and take a role in helping to keep the name of Llanelli RFC alive. It's proven to be very challenging and I knew that it would be the case, but I'm very hopeful of securing its name in the top echelons of Welsh rugby once more.

Llanelli, as a name in world rugby, is famous. Wherever I have gone, whatever part of the world I was in, when someone asked me who I had played for, and I had said Llanelli, they knew straightaway what I was talking about. The fear was that we were finding it more difficult to find people to volunteer and support Llanelli as a town team – we were fishing in the same pond as the regional Scarlets side.

Stradey Park had gone – that was unavoidable – but all

the history and heritage must live on in the memory and we need to ensure that Llanelli RFC continues to play and make new memories for the current generation of players and supporters.

The major hurdle in our goal, unsurprisingly, was when the WRU took the controversial step of downgrading the Premier Division clubs to being classed as community clubs, which significantly cut their budgets.

It's an ongoing project and I'm likely to be involved for as long as it takes. Nothing is guaranteed for life; things happen, and rugby is challenging, not least the finances. Rupert Moon and Gareth are now Heritage Directors and we have introduced guardians, or vice presidents of Llanelli, through which people can donate to help the club.

CHAPTER 14

Journey's End

PLAYING RUGBY HAS given me a tremendous perspective on the world through providing so many opportunities to travel, firstly with Llanelli and Wales as a player, and then as a member of World Rugby. It even led to myself and Alana being invited to a garden party at Buckingham Palace to meet royalty. It was a real surprise and I was never quite able to work out how it had happened.

The most bizarre invite I ever received, on the back of rugby, was to visit the Circuit de Nevers Magny-Cours Grand Prix on 1 July 2007, just before the Rugby World Cup in France. The phone call from Jonathan Griffiths, the Llanelli scrum-half, came out of the blue. If that wasn't surreal enough, he went on to ask whether I could bring my Welsh jersey with me and help put a rugby pack together. He added that we could bring our wives along, and a chauffeur would pick us up from Charles de Gaulle Airport. I accepted, not quite sure of what I was letting myself in for. I immediately rang Laurance but he was going away. However, I managed to get international players John Davies and Huw Williams-Jones on board.

We flew over and were met by a chauffeur who drove us to Magny-Cours where we were put up in a château which was out of this world. After we had settled in, the phone went and the organiser said, 'Can you come to the race track by 7 o'clock on Friday evening?' Which we all did, along with our wives.

Once there we were directed upstairs to a large function room which overlooked the starting grid, to find a crowd of around 200 invited guests sipping champagne. On arriving I was met by Steve Rider from the BBC who was the evening's presenter. He said, 'Anthony, you're a brave man to do what you're about to do.'

I replied, 'I haven't a clue what I'm about to do!'

'They haven't told you?'

'No!'

'It's scrummaging,' he said.

'Scrummaging?' I asked, perplexed. Then eight guys turned up carrying a big green carpet which they then rolled out. I noticed one of the top French referees along with the French coach. They called us over and said, 'You scrummage.' They had also invited players from Italy and France who were as equally perplexed. We were all bemused but formed ourselves into a scrum formation, Huw Williams-Jones, John and myself made up the front row, along with Jonathan and some other players from the UK and Ireland.

The referee then told us to engage and blew his whistle. The French coach appeared with the ball and fed the scrum. Smash! We were caught off-guard and driven back. After a quick get-together, we all decided to take it seriously. We really had a go at them in the second scrum. It was crazy looking back, people could have got hurt.

Then the various Formula 1 pit crews – Red Bull, Mercedes, Renault – appeared in their company shirts and the announcer declared, 'The competition is for seven tickets for the Rugby World Cup final.' We all turned to each other and said, 'We have a good chance of winning this!' But then he said, 'Anthony, thank you very much for the demonstration. You will be with Red Bull.' We were basically there to coach and were assigned a team each and were given a few minutes to form them into packs and get them ready for scrummaging.

The crews were really up for it and ultra competitive, which

I suppose was to be expected when you consider they were at the elite end of their sport. They also, naturally, wanted to beat their rival teams.

The teams were called together and the competition proper started. It was an unbelievable spectacle which could only happen in France. They piled into one another, shirts were ripped off and fights broke out left, right and centre! The referee just let it go – a typical French ref! I was amazed that no one got injured.

It all ended with everyone absolutely delighted with the 'entertainment'.

The organisers thanked us profusely and we were returned to the château. The following morning our chauffeur arrived to take us to watch the Grand Prix practice session at a prime spot. Then we were given a tour of the pits – I could never have been a racing driver as I couldn't even fit my leg in those cockpits!

That evening we were invited to a concert before attending the race itself the following day. We were greeted by the boss of Formula 1 and I presented him with my Welsh jersey and thanked him for his hospitality and such an incredible experience.

Whoever came up with the concept of a scrum contest was a genius and it was a refreshing change not to have the backs around! But then again, that's France for you, they really value their packs.

*

Having previously played for the Fijian Barbarians I was delighted to be asked to play for the original legendary Baa-Baas invitation team. My first outing in the famous black-and-white hooped shirt was against Leicester up at Welfare Road. It was a full house and I was reunited with Des Fitzgerald, playing on the same side for once.

I then did two Easter tours in Wales with them. The tradition, stretching back decades, was to play Penarth on the Good Friday, Swansea on the Saturday, and Cardiff on the Bank Holiday Monday – you would usually play in two of the three games. The games would always attract a bumper crowd and the rugby never failed to entertain. Sadly, those Easter tours have become another victim of professionalism, having been declared surplus to requirements in the professional era.

At least the tradition of the Barbarians is still alive, with regular international matches each year. It's important that people get to see rugby being played away from the shackles of the pressure to win. I always found it a privilege and was really chuffed to have had the honour of playing for the Barbarians with all its history of flair and attacking intent.

*

I also played for a Willie Anderson XV over in Omagh, Northern Ireland, in the late '80s, at the height of the 'Troubles'. It was a real experience, although not one I enjoyed at times. The locals' sense of humour was great, however. When I arrived and stepped out of the small, propeller-driven plane, Willie Anderson said to me, 'Buck, you're looking a bit pale. Just keep running around; they haven't shot a moving target in years.'

Mark Ring and myself were then driven by car to the ground. It was bleak in places and a bit nervy. I overheard someone say, 'The Brits are in.' I thought to myself, 'I better not stay here for very long.' There was always that fear but they looked after us very well. The welcome was just as warm as in other places, and you got the feeling that they appreciated you making the effort to come and play. That is the magic of rugby, it helps cross divides.

*

The Fijian Barbarians were invited to tour South Africa and they asked whether I would like to join them. The offer came with quite a substantial payment, as South Africa were desperate to break the embargo brought about in protest at the country's apartheid laws. While the offer was tempting, I decided to turn them down. Besides, my father-in-law was a big trade unionist with strong beliefs, and would have been really critical of me if I even considered going.

*

I never did get to play for Wales at home on the Arms Park, which was disappointing. Having said that, I achieved my ambition of playing for my country – even if I had only won one cap I would have been just as delighted. There are plenty of great players who never get the opportunity to pull on their country's jersey.

As it turned out, I played five times for Wales, and to face New Zealand, Australia, England, Ireland and Tonga is an amazing achievement. Four of those games came in the Rugby World Cup and the history books will tell you that we remain Wales' highest placed side in that tournament. In fairness, the game has changed dramatically since then and I think the World Cup has given rugby a massive focus and something to get us all excited about every four years. We were a bunch of amateurs and the tournament was in its infancy. Saying that, I will always be proud of what we achieved, to play in a World Cup is the pinnacle of your sport and I was extremely fortunate that fate conspired to place me in the right place at the right time to help my country do so well. For that I will be eternally grateful.

*

As for my time as team manager of the Scarlets, when I think back to all that the side achieved, I really did feel a part of it, especially with all the effort, hard work and preparation which had gone into being successful. As I've said, you were never acknowledged on the same level as the players, which is as it should be, but you still took a great deal of satisfaction from it all. I shared in the emotion of it. I always felt we had a great history and that people were very complimentary about our style of play.

Our experiences in Europe were one of the main contributors to the success of the national side. We were getting used to the travelling and were becoming successful on the road. We had come a long way from just jumping on a bus and travelling down the road to play a game. We had made two semi-finals – missing out by the narrowest of margins on both occasions – and had become a highly respected and worthy opponent for any side. With so many local players involved, this all helped our national cause.

The last ten years have been one of the most successful periods in our history when it comes to the national side. We have been winning Six Nations Championships, Triple Crowns and Grand Slams – but can it be sustained? I was often asked that question on my travels around the world. In many ways, being smaller has made us more efficient. Team Wales has almost become a regional team.

Personally, I think it's going to be a big ask to continue that run of success. As a rugby playing nation, we're too small and need to invest a lot of money which we haven't got. We're basically based around a 70-mile stretch of the M4 corridor. The Scarlets are 13 miles away from the Ospreys, the Dragons are even closer to the Blues. We are competing against so many other sports and interests to attract crowds and the next generation of players. I'm not sure what the answer is – perhaps plough more money into the community game to introduce youngsters to the sport?

We need people with the very best interests of the game at heart to make the right decisions. We all need to rally round and support our clubs, which are the very foundation of Welsh rugby. This is where the next generation starts, in the clubs. We ignore, at our peril, the core game in Wales.

*

One of the most unexpected twists in my rugby journey has been my involvement with the referees. When the appointment came around I wasn't really sure what to expect, as up to that point I had very little involvement with referees, other than being at the opposite end of their whistle on the pitch. As it turned out, I thoroughly enjoyed the time spent working with them and seeing their role from a different perspective. Understanding the terminology and how they approach refereeing the game, against how others see the game and how people play the game – there are so many variables to consider.

I don't think the wider public appreciates them enough – I certainly didn't give them much consideration until I got involved with World Rugby. I had never really had any involvement with any referee, other than having a few beers with Derek Bevan who I always saw as a good guy and enjoyed his company.

*

In a way, I owe all that I have achieved in the game to my wife, Alana. If she had not been behind that bar at Ystradgynlais Rugby Club all those years ago, I may never have taken up the sport and this journey would not have been possible. I have so much to be grateful for with all the opportunities rugby has given me. It has been amazing. Moving up into the front row was a real shift in attitude – it didn't make me a tough guy but I had to become mentally strong to compete in that environment.

I have been asked whether I regretted not playing rugby sooner. The truth is, I don't know how good I could have been if I had played the game from a younger age. It was what it was. I don't have any regrets – ten years of playing first-class rugby and representing your country is a pretty good innings for anyone.

What I wanted to do more than anything was to get to the highest level that I could. I never wanted to be one of those people sitting in the club saying, 'I could have played for Swansea, I could have played for Llanelli or I could have played for Neath.' I wanted to be sitting there and able to say, 'I had a go.'

I never wanted people to think that I was some special rugby player. I just want people to believe that dreams can come true when you really put the effort in. I also know that I had a bit of luck along the way. I was in the right place at the right time – I know so many good players who just didn't get the break. I genuinely believe that in any walk of life you always need that bit of luck. I was also fortunate in that I never really struggled with injuries.

I had opportunities and I took them. That's all you can do – if someone offers you an opportunity, take it. There's no shame in failing, the shame lies in never giving it a go.

And it was opportunity which brought me back full circle to be able to help out with Ystradgynlais, and later the chance to go back and help Llanelli – both clubs offered me so much and it was nice to be able to give something back in return.

Finally, I'm hoping that the proceeds of this book will help, in some small way, to secure the future of the playing fields in Ystradgynlais which are so important to the community. It's terrific to go down there on a Sunday morning and see all the youngsters running around enjoying the game we all love so much. I hope that one day my grandsons, Fletcher and

Otis, will enjoy those facilities and who knows become future internationals! I just hope that their journeys will turn out to be as memorable as mine.

Testimonials

ALTHOUGH WE BOTH played in the inaugural Rugby World Cup in New Zealand in 1987, I have to be honest and admit that I don't remember him! There is no doubt our paths would have crossed but more than likely they would be in some ale house in Wellington or Auckland and, with lots of alcohol consumed, I could have been speaking to anybody.

Roll forward three decades and Wales elected a new member to represent them on World Rugby and it was their former prop Anthony Buchanan, who I just couldn't picture. My first impressions as he walked through the door to the first meeting were his barrel chest and his huge smile.

I immediately liked the cut of his jib, as his contributions at that first meeting, although limited, were pertinent and to the point. Over the years, he added more and more to the meetings and all his comments were based on the game of rugby and not politics.

It was in the bar after that I really got to know Bucks, though! He was always the first to the bar and that infectious smile brought everyone into his circle. He had a story for every occasion and grew into one of the most popular characters in World Rugby, respected by everyone around the globe.

To be honest, I threw him a curve ball at his first meeting by asking him to chair the Referee Selection Committee, and whilst saying he thought it out of his expertise, he threw himself wholeheartedly into the role and gained the respect of the refereeing community for his honesty and frankness. He took what is normally a poisoned chalice, and delivered the best ever refereeing performance at the 2019 RWC – what an outstanding achievement (and from a prop!).

More importantly, I got to know Bucks the person and what fun that has been. His huge infectious smile does not lie, and it's always a pleasure to have our 'pre-meeting sessions' in the pub the night before our meetings, although on occasions they did tend to drift into the wee small hours. It doesn't matter where we were in the world, he would sniff out an appropriate venue where we could sample the local brew and chew the fat.

When I switched my phone on having come through security at the airport, it inevitably pinged with a message from Bucks asking, 'Have you arrived yet? I'm in the pub around the corner from the hotel!'

Most of us on the rugby political scene probably hang around too long, but it is a mark of the man that Bucks got out when he wanted to and wasn't voted out of post.

All in all, he's just a Top Man. It's been a pleasure to get to know Bucks and his wife Alana, and enjoy their company on our varied sojourns over the years and I will miss my phone not pinging when I come through security!

John Jeffrey
Scotland and British and Irish Lions

It's refreshing to see a biography from this era and it's important to show the present generation what the game was like in the amateur days before the advent of professional and regional rugby. The game has changed so much over the last 30 years and Anthony Buchanan is well placed to comment as he was right at the heart of it all for so long as a player, team manager and administrator.

I first recall Bucks from when I was a youngster growing

up in the Gwendraeth Valley supporting Llanelli RFC with friends. He was a hard-working, no-nonsense front rower who always put a shift in around the field as well as in the scrums, and became one of the favourites down at Stradey Park. He has quite rightly earned his place amongst the Scarlet legends.

I can also remember him playing for Wales. He never let his country down and arguably should have won more caps.

I got to know him personally as a referee, when he became team manager, first with the Scarlets and then his beloved Llanelli RFC. I realised just how knowledgeable and passionate he was about the game. We would often have chats over coffee and discuss the sport we both love. Later, when he became a member of World Rugby, we would sometimes travel up to London together and he was always terrific company. He never had any hidden agenda and he always put his heart and soul into helping protect and enhance the game he obviously cares so much about.

I felt very humbled and honoured when he chose to fly out to Fiji in 2016 to present me with my cap for breaking the then world record for refereeing the most international rugby matches.

Bucks has given so much back to rugby – not least to Ystradgynlais, his home town club that he has never forgotten. Llanelli, the Scarlets, Wales and the world of rugby in general owe him a huge debt of gratitude.

Diolch yn fawr iawn i ti Anthony.

Nigel Owens MBE

Anthony refused to play rugby at school, which shows you he must have been a strong-willed youngster to stand up to his sports teacher in a rugby dominated school, and only took up the game when he was 22.

He had the perfect physique for a prop forward and became an all-round ball player. His handling skills no doubt benefited from his time as a goalkeeper, at a time when most props just did the basics of scrummaging and lineouts.

Although he played during an era when rugby was very physical, and frequently very dirty, he always played within the laws of the game and was seldom sent off.

On retirement from playing he became a team manager and was held in high esteem by all players before being appointed a member of the Welsh Rugby Union and distinguishing himself as an administrator of the game with World Rugby. He spent a lot of time on the development of the game, which is a hell of a thing to ask a prop forward to do!

It gave me great pleasure seeing Anthony, as a fellow Cwmtwrch boy, graduate through the ranks of Ystradgynlais, Llanelli and Wales, always with a smile on his face, and I am honoured to be able to consider him a close friend.

Clive Rowlands OBE
Wales

I first met Anthony Buchanan when I was a young 19 year old stepping out from Welsh youth rugby on my path to senior rugby with Swansea. At that time I had no idea how our paths would cross and how our friendship would grow. As a tight-head – he was a loose-head – we played against each other on several occasions and had a mutual respect. We toured the South Sea Islands and played together in the inaugural World Cup where we packed down in the front row against Tonga for his first cap.

Bucks came to rugby late but packed in the years of missed rugby experience and games with total passion and energy. Without doubt Bucks had a great rugby engine that gave him the ability to play a really expansive, ball-handling game of rugby for a prop in the late '80s, like a New Zealand forward of the day.

We trained together, having been paired by Clive Rowlands as training partners. My expertise was weights and his was running. I remember on one occasion we ran past a church in Ystradgynlais, and Clive Rowlands appeared from behind the bushes to give us encouragement!

He was funny and a great team man who always had time for everybody on and off the pitch. He also liked a pint, along with a few old stories and jokes after games. He's a big family man off the field – I really saw this first-hand when we shared a room in New Zealand for Bucks' first cap against Tonga at the 1987 Rugby World Cup. He was so proud to be playing for Wales, and just wished his family were there to see him achieve his goal.

On the pitch he was a different man and stood his ground, backing his teammates in uncomfortable and violent games. He always played with a smile on his face and respected the opposition and played hard but fair. No wonder he went on to be a coach, team manager and work with World Rugby because he had the gift of the gab! He could mix with paupers and princes and deserved every accolade he achieved over his rugby career.

Bucks never forgot where he was born and bred and his lovely family and friends. You could take the boy out of Ystradgynlais but you could never take Ystradgynlais out of the boy wherever he went in the world.

Thanks Butty, top prop.

Stuart Evans
Swansea, Neath and Wales

When I first met Anthony he was courting my sister who used to work behind the bar at Ystradgynlais RFC, and he was a football player. He really fitted in well socially and became part of our social circle, coming to the club on Saturday nights with Alana.

We didn't have much in common until the day, a few years down the line, when he announced that he was going to give rugby a go! As with all players, he started with the seconds but soon took to the game and, to my astonishment, people in selection were starting to mention him for a first-team place. This was quite a step-up considering the short time he had been playing the game. We were playing in Section A in west Wales, which was an extremely competitive and physical league, but he took to it very well and established himself as a first-choice player very quickly, to my surprise.

I was very much a person who was committed to playing for Ystradgynlais, having played more than 620 games. Anthony started to fit in as a key part of our pack. At one stage he had hurt his ribs and ruled himself out of playing a key game. As you can tell, my commitment was total, so I had every liniment and strapping available to keep me playing on Saturdays. I visited my supplier and it was recommended that Anthony use a liniment which may have been used on horses at one point! Dropping it off at his house in the morning, the instructions for use were somewhat discoloured. He placed the liniment directly on the injury, which resulted in burns to his rib cage being the reason for not playing!

The turning point came when first-class teams were showing interest, which was good for him but not so good for Ystradgynlais. When he approached me and the club and said that he had been asked to change position to loose-head prop, I actually told him that he would not make a prop as long as he had a hole in his backside. I soon discovered that his determination to give this a go would prove me wrong. During one of the last training sessions we had we went head-to-head, and after the scrummaging session I told him that I believed he could make it.

The rest, as they say, is history. What an achievement from a round ball player! To go on from that to work in administration at the top end, including the Welsh Rugby Union and World Rugby, also earned my respect.

Kevin Edwards
Ystradgynlais and Brecknockshire County

Geraint Thomas is a former WalesOnline journalist who was shortlisted for the 2016 News Reporter of the Year at the Media Wales Awards.

His first book for Y Lolfa, *Terry Davies: Wales's First Superstar Fullback*, also a rugby autobiography, was very well received and was shortlisted for the 2017 Cross Sports Book of the Year Awards.

He repeated the feat in 2020 when his second rugby biography, *Glenn Webbe: The Gloves are Off*, was shortlisted in the renamed Telegraph Sports Book Awards.

Also from Y Lolfa:

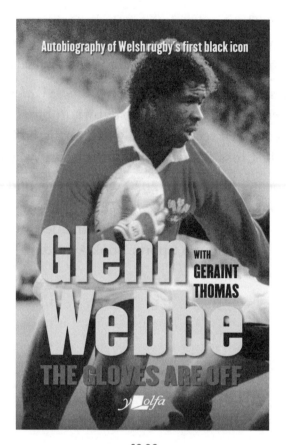

£9.99

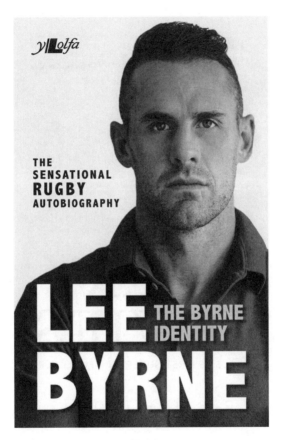

yLolfa

THE
SENSATIONAL
RUGBY
AUTOBIOGRAPHY

LEE
THE BYRNE
IDENTITY
BYRNE

£9.99

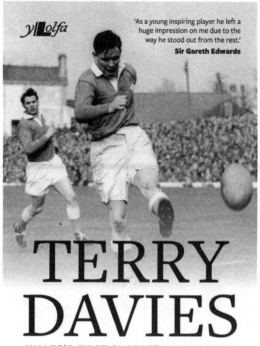

'As a young inspiring player he left a huge impression on me due to the way he stood out from the rest.'

Sir Gareth Edwards

TERRY DAVIES

WALES'S FIRST SUPERSTAR FULLBACK

WITH

GERAINT THOMAS

£9.99

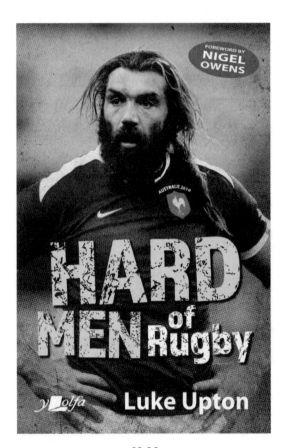

LYNN DAVIES

hard men
of WELSH
RUGBY

Y Lolfa

£7.95

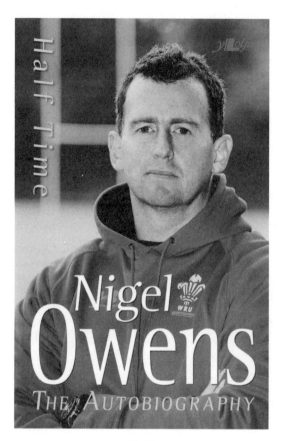

Half Time

Nigel
Owens

THE AUTOBIOGRAPHY

£9.95